# The Kitchen Table

A CULINARY JOURNEY AROUND THE WORLD

# The Kitchen Table

### A CULINARY JOURNEY AROUND THE WORLD

VIKING

Karine milking a goat to make
Norwegian *gjetost* (goat cheese)

# WELCOME TO THE KITCHEN TABLE

Exploring destinations and discovering different cultures and traditions is at the heart of every Viking river and ocean journey. And of course food – not only the recipes prepared by our onboard chefs, but local cuisine in all the fascinating places our ships visit – is an essential part of the overall Viking experience.

We created this book in response to requests from our guests, who told us how much they enjoyed the food served on board our ships, and in the ports of call, and wanted to try making some of these dishes at home.

On the following pages you will find some of our favorite recipes from Scandinavia, Western and Eastern Europe, Asia, North America and the Caribbean, inspired by our travels and yours. It is a food odyssey, and a celebration of all the wonderful flavors you can savor while traveling the world.

My grandmother and best friend Ragnhild (Mamsen) Hagen inspired my own love of life's basics and nature as well as home cooked food. Sincere and honest, Mamsen was hardworking and liked to keep things simple. I learned the most basic cooking skills from her, and I infuse these – and their simplicity – in every dish I cook.

All of the recipes in the book are easy to follow, simple and delicious. I hope you enjoy making them at home and bringing bits of the world home from our kitchen tables to yours.

Velkommen til bords!

Karine Hagen
**Sr. Vice President**
**Viking Cruises**

From 793 until 1066, Scandinavian Norsemen explored Europe by its
seas and rivers for trade, raids and conquest...

# THE VIKINGS

The Vikings were not just warriors, traders and craftsmen, they were also the ultimate
explorers; the Old Norse verb "to Viking" means to go on a waterborne journey whether by
river or sea. Their routes stretched from the Artic north of Norway, along the Atlantic coasts of
France and Spain to the Mediterranean; they explored the waterways of Russia and Ukraine to
reach Byzantium (now Istanbul); and linked eastwards to the Islamic territories.

The Viking Age began with a raid on the abbey on the island of Lindisfarne, off the northeast
coast of England, in 793 AD. Today, in the church near the ruined abbey, you can read a
formal apology for the bloodshed, which was offered by a Norwegian bishop in 1993.

Their sphere of activity extended far beyond their homelands in Scandinavia and the adjacent
coastal lands around the Baltic Sea, reaching not only the northern tip of Europe but also its
western, southern and eastern limits.

Ships were central to Viking activities, the descendants of millennia of nautical experience.
Scandinavia's extensive coastline made the sea the preferred route; in fact Norway took
its name from this natural sea route – the name Norway comes from the Old Norse word
*norðrvegr*, which means "northern way."

Viking ships had figureheads at the stem and stern designed to scare their enemies. But
sea battles were rare, and even then were fought close to shore. The Vikings' aim was
not to destroy their enemies' ships, but to capture them if possible, as they represented a
considerable investment in time, resources and labor.

The Vikings traded all over Europe, and as far east as Central Asia. They bought silver, silk,
spices, walnuts, wine, jewelry, glass and pottery, and sold honey, tin, wheat, wool, wood, iron,
fur, leather, fish and walrus ivory.

Their diet was designed to sustain their lifestyle. At sea, they would eat dried or salted meat
or fish, washed down with beer or sour milk. At home, they farmed crops and raised animals.

Throughout Viking Age Scandinavia, almost everyone's main preoccupation was the production of food. Farming, together with fishing, trapping and collecting, were the main activities in the annual cycle. Communities had to be largely self-sufficient, taking advantage of fertile soils and good pasture. As a result, crab apples, plums and cherries were all part of the Viking diet, as were rose hips and raspberries, wild strawberries, blackberries, elderberries, rowan, hawthorn and various other wild berries. Hazelnuts grew wild and were a favorite.

Well-stocked fishing grounds meant oysters, mussels and shrimps were eaten in large quantities, and cod and salmon were popular fish. Seals were hunted nearly everywhere, while in Norway's southern regions herring was also important.

Milk came from cows, goats and sheep, and fermented milk products like skyr or surmjölk, both similar to yogurt, were produced, as well as butter and cheese.

On a typical day the Viking people would eat two meals. Breakfast – the dagmal, or day meal – was served an hour after rising: they might have some stew leftover from the night before, served with bread and milk; porridge and dried fruit and buttermilk with bread were also popular.

The nattmal, or night meal, was eaten at the end of the working day and would be fish or meat stewed with vegetables. For a sweet treat they might have dried fruit with honey (honey was the only sweetener available to them).

Using barley, rye and oats, the Vikings made beer, stews and porridge. Breads were baked on flat stones or iron griddles over the fire, while meats such as beef, pork, mutton, chicken and occasionally horsemeat, and vegetables – cabbage, onions, garlic, leeks, turnips, peas and beans – were cooked over the hearth, or firepit.

They drank ale, mead (a strong, fermented drink made from honey), bjórr (a strong fruit wine) or buttermilk daily.

Today, many of their culinary traditions endure, not only throughout Scandinavia but also in the areas in which they settled, including savory game such as venison served with berries; sauerkraut; porridge and exotic spices including cinnamon, cardamom, star anise and ginger.

The Viking legacy can also be found in the Scandinavian origins of place-names; and in Iceland, they left behind their literature, the Icelandic sagas, celebrating the greatest victories of their glorious past.

"To move, to breathe, to fly, to float,
To gain all while you give,
To roam the roads of lands remote,
To travel is to live."

Hans Christian Andersen

# CONTENTS

# SCANDINAVIA

Scandinavia yields some of the most delicious, varied and healthy cuisine in the world, from the fjords of Norway to the Swedish archipelago. The history of Scandinavian food dates back to the time of the Vikings, who sourced much of their cuisine from the North Sea, and were particularly fond of cod, mussels and cured salmon. Today, several dishes and ingredients link all the regions of Scandinavia together, bringing the Nordic food experience to life. Scandinavian cooking is all about quality, attention to detail and simplicity, where the main ingredient flavors the dish. Hearty dishes such as pork and meatballs contrast with exquisitely presented open sandwiches and smörgåsbord. Cured fish and herring are also popular, as are berries, including lingonberries, cloudberries and blueberries. A shot of aquavit, a distinct eau de vie flavored with caraway, is an important part of Scandinavian culture.

# NORWAY

With its spectacular mountains, wilderness and coast, and an abundance of fresh produce available, including seafood and game, Norwegian cuisine is diverse, and usually quite unfussy – letting the natural ingredients speak for themselves.

Mamsen's, the popular Norwegian-style deli on board our Viking ships, is well loved for its traditional Scandinavian fare, and the waffles based on my grandmother's recipes are legendary. Serve with jam or Norwegian brown goat's cheese, or both, and savor a flavor of authentic Norway.

# MAMSEN'S WAFFLES

**Serves 4 – 6**

8.8 oz (250g) all purpose
   (plain) flour
2 tbsp sugar
2 eggs
10 fl oz (300ml) milk
3 oz (90g) butter
Pinch ground cardamom
½ tsp vanilla extract

1 In a bowl, mix together the flour, sugar, eggs and milk to make a smooth batter.

2 In a small saucepan, gently melt the butter, then whisk into the batter along with the cardamom and vanilla.

3 Cook with a waffle iron or lightly oil a grill pan, heat to medium and cook 4 to 5 tablespoons of the mixture per waffle. Cook the waffle until bubbles start to form on the surface, then flip over and cook until both sides are golden brown.

My father and Viking Chairman Torstein Hagen does not like spending time on unimportant decisions. Which includes his choice of wardrobe: one style of shirt, and one style of suit. And his choice of favorite food: poached salmon, cucumber salad and boiled potatoes. If he could only eat this for the rest of his life he would be a happy man. Here he is showing our corporate chef how to properly marinate the cucumber slices to prevent them from becoming soggy!

# CHAIRMAN'S CHOICE: POACHED SALMON & CUCUMBER SALAD

**Serves 4**

4 salmon fillets
(around 6 oz/170g)

FOR THE PICKLED CUCUMBER:
1 cucumber
Salt
2 tbsp sugar
3 ½ fl oz (100ml) water
8 ½ fl oz (250ml) rice wine
    vinegar

FOR THE CHIVE SAUCE:
1 pint (475ml) heavy
    (double) cream
2 ¾ oz (80g) butter
Salt and pepper
1 tbsp fresh chives

**1** Peel the cucumber and slice into discs. Sprinkle the discs with salt and allow to marinate for 5 minutes. Squeeze out the liquid. Mix the sugar, water and vinegar, pour over the sliced cucumber, and place in the fridge for half an hour. Drain and reserve.

**2** Bring a pan of salted water to a boil, then turn down the heat and add the salmon fillets. Allow to poach for about 8 minutes until just tender.

**3** Meanwhile, prepare the chive sauce. Bring the cream to the boil in a saucepan, then reduce the heat and allow to simmer until reduced by half. Whisk in the butter, then add the fresh chives and season to taste.

Roasted pork belly or *ribbe* is a traditional Christmas dish in Oslo and in south and east Norway. The real test to a great *ribbe* is getting the *"svor"* (crackling) right, and making sure it is scored properly.

# ROASTED PORK BELLY

**Serves 4**

2.2 lb (1kg) pork belly
  (rind on)
Salt and pepper
2 red onions
1 whole head of garlic
Thumb-sized piece of ginger
2 bay leaves
Just over 2 pints (1 liter) water

FOR THE CABBAGE STEW:
8 slices streaky smoked bacon
1 head cabbage
4 tbsp all purpose
  (plain) flour
1 tbsp caraway seeds
4 fl oz (120 ml) white vinegar
1 ¾ oz (50g) granulated
  sugar

FOR THE GRAVY:
3 ½ oz (100g) butter
3-4 tbsp all purpose
  (plain) flour

**1** Preheat the oven to 425°F (220°C). Place the pork belly on a board, skin side up. Score the meat diagonally in both directions to create a diamond pattern, about an inch apart with a very sharp knife through the skin into the fat but avoiding the meat. Season both sides of the meat with salt and pepper, and rub in.

**2** Quarter the red onions, slice the head of garlic in half and cut the ginger into slices (there is no need to peel anything). Scatter them into the roasting pan with the bay leaves and place the seasoned meat skin side down on top of the vegetables.

**3** Add the water and cover with aluminium foil. Lower the heat to 350°F (175°C), then cook for 1 ½ to 2 hours.

**4** Meanwhile, make the cabbage stew. Lay two or three slices of bacon in the bottom of a large casserole dish. Cover with a layer of shredded cabbage, sprinkle with a light dusting of flour and a pinch of caraway seeds, then season with salt and pepper. Repeat the layering process until you run out of room.

**5** Gently pour water into the pot until it's about three-quarters full. Bring to the boil, then cook for about 45 minutes to an hour, stirring occasionally, until the cabbage is soft. Allow to cool slightly, then stir in the vinegar. Add the sugar gradually to taste.

**6** Take the pork out of the oven and place onto a rack or gridiron skin side up, making sure that there is still liquid in the pan so that the meat doesn't dry out. Turn the oven back up to 425°F (220°C) and roast for about half an hour until the skin has started to puff up, then turn back down to 350°F (175°C) and leave to roast for a final hour, checking occasionally to make sure the skin isn't burning. The meat should now be meltingly tender. Carefully remove it to a chopping board, cover with foil and leave to rest while you make the gravy.

**7** In a saucepan, melt the butter, then add 3 tablespoons of flour. Heat gently, stirring until the paste thickens. Add the juices from the tray, stirring until smooth. Bring to the boil and simmer, stirring constantly for a few minutes. Finally, pour the gravy through a sieve before serving.

When the leaves start turning, Norwegians start getting hungry for fårikål! This popular dish is traditionally made with bone-in lamb or mutton, stewed with cabbage and served with boiled potatoes and the delicious cooking broth. The peppercorns are usually left in the finished dish, and add welcome bursts of fire to this great comfort food. Go for a long Sunday walk in the forest, and work up an appetite for this iconic Norwegian dish.

# LAMB FÅRIKÅL

### Serves 4 – 6

2.2 lb (1kg) lamb shoulder
Large green cabbage
2-3 tsp salt
15 black peppercorns
Around 1 pint (475ml) water

**1** Cut the lamb shoulder into 3cm slices (if you want to keep the bone in, ask your butcher to slice the lamb for you).

**2** Cut the cabbage into quarters down to the core, then cut each quarter into 3 or 4 wedges, keeping part of the core on each segment to hold the leaves together.

**3** Place a layer of lamb, then a layer of cabbage into a heavy casserole dish, seasoning each layer with salt and sprinkling over some of the peppercorns. Repeat the layering process until all the ingredients are used up, finishing with a layer of cabbage.

**4** Pour over the water and bring to the boil. Turn down the heat, then simmer gently for 2 to 3 hours until the lamb is very tender, occasionally checking the water level to prevent the dish from boiling dry.

# SWEDEN

Swedish cuisine offers a range of tantalizing tastes. Cheese, breads, meatballs (served with lingonberry jam) and potatoes – usually mashed or boiled – are all popular. Whatever they are doing, the Swedes make time to stop for a morning coffee and sweet roll in a tradition known as *fika*, and they invented smörgåsbord, the delicious buffet of hot and cold dishes popular around the world.

This classic Swedish dish features traditional Scandinavian spicing. Serve the meatballs with mashed or boiled potatoes and lingonberry jam. Garnish with chopped parsley.

# MEATBALLS

## Serves 4 - 6

Olive oil
1 large white onion
1 lb (450g) minced beef
1 lb (450g) minced pork
3 oz (85g) panko
   breadcrumbs
2 eggs, separated
5 fl oz (150ml) milk
½ tsp allspice
½ tsp ground nutmeg
Salt and pepper

FOR THE GRAVY:
2 tbsp butter
2 tbsp all purpose (plain) flour
1 pint (475ml) chicken or veal
   stock
4 fl oz (120ml) heavy
   (double) cream
Parsley

1 Heat one tablespoon of olive oil in a large frying pan. Finely chop the onion, then cook gently until translucent.

2 In a large bowl, combine the minced beef, minced pork, breadcrumbs, egg yolks, milk, allspice, nutmeg and cooked onion. Season with salt and pepper. Mix well with clean hands, then roll the mixture into golf ball-sized meatballs.

3 Add a further tablespoon of olive oil to the pan, then cook the meatballs in batches, taking care not to crowd the pan, until all sides are brown. Transfer to a plate.

4 In a clean pan, melt the butter, then add the flour and whisk for one to two minutes until pale and bubbling. Add the stock slowly, whisking constantly. Bring to the boil, then turn down the heat and add the cream. Return the meatballs to the pan and cook for a further 10 minutes, stirring occasionally.

5 Serve immediately with mashed or boiled potatoes, a spoonful of lingonberry jam and a sprinkling of chopped parsley.

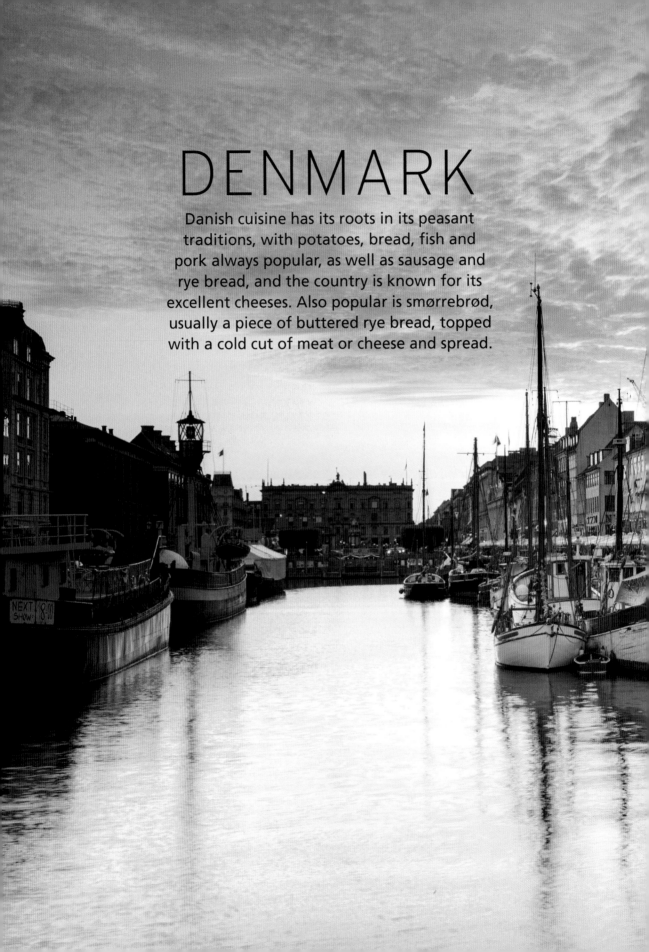

# DENMARK

Danish cuisine has its roots in its peasant traditions, with potatoes, bread, fish and pork always popular, as well as sausage and rye bread, and the country is known for its excellent cheeses. Also popular is smørrebrød, usually a piece of buttered rye bread, topped with a cold cut of meat or cheese and spread.

Open sandwiches are popular across all the Scandinavian countries. One slice of bread, often dark whole-grain rye, is topped with various combinations of cured meats, fish, vegetables or cheese and topped with a range of condiments. Ida Davidson is considered the Danish Queen of Smørrebrød and here she is showing me how to make her favorite: simple lard with potatoes and chives, proving that sometimes the simplest flavors are the best!

# OPEN SANDWICHES (SMØRREBRØD)

**SALMON GRAVLAX ON RYE BREAD WITH MUSTARD DILL SAUCE**

FOR THE SALMON GRAVLAX:
3 tbsp salt
1 tbsp sugar
1 shot vodka
1 lemon, zested
1 tbsp fresh dill, chopped
1 salmon fillet with skin on, around 6 oz (170g)

FOR THE OPEN SANDWICH:
4 slices dark rye bread
Butter
Mixed salad leaves

FOR THE SAUCE:
3 tbsp Dijon mustard
1 tbsp honey
1 tbsp cider vinegar
1 tbsp olive oil
1 tbsp fresh dill, chopped

**1** For the salmon gravlax, mix the salt, sugar, vodka, lemon zest and dill together in a bowl. Place the salmon fillet on a shallow dish and cover completely with the marinade. Cover and refrigerate overnight.

**2** To make the open sandwiches, lightly toast each slice of bread, then butter and top with salad leaves, then thin slices of the salmon gravlax. Mix all the mustard dill sauce ingredients together and drizzle over each sandwich. Garnish with fresh dill and a lemon wedge.

ALTERNATIVE TOPPINGS
Classic toppings include Danish blue cheese paired with tart raspberries and redcurrants, and beef carbonade: a seared beef patty served with an onion confit. Beef tartare is another favorite: raw, finely ground beef tenderloin is served with condiments including capers, chopped red onion, cornichons and a raw egg yolk.

# FINLAND

Finland is known for its magnificent
forests and lakes. Salmon and herring are
staple foods, as well as deer and moose.
Arctic wild berries, including cloudberries,
are also popular.

The Finnish take their cinnamon buns very seriously – there's even a National Cinnamon Roll Day. Although the recipe is similar in several Scandinavian countries, the shape of Korvapuusti (literally 'slapped ear') is unique to Finland. Sprinkling generously with pearl sugar before baking is essential.

# KORVAPUUSTI (CINNAMON AND CARDAMOM BUNS)

## Makes 15 – 20 rolls

FOR THE DOUGH:
1 lb (450g) strong white
   bread flour
2 tsp salt
2.5 oz (70g) sugar
1 x 7g sachet instant dried
   yeast
2 tsp ground cardamom
   (preferably freshly ground)
5 fl oz (150ml) milk
5 fl oz (150ml) water
2 oz (55g) butter

FOR THE FILLING:
4 oz (115g) soft butter
6 tbsp sugar
1 tbsp cinnamon

TO DECORATE:
Pearl (nibbed) sugar

1 Place the flour into a large bowl, then stir in the salt, sugar, dried yeast and cardamom.

2 In a small saucepan, warm the milk, water and butter over a low heat until the butter has just melted, then turn off the heat and allow to cool to room temperature.

3 Pour most of the milk mixture into the dry ingredients and stir with a knife until it forms a light, sticky dough. Reserve any leftover liquid for brushing over the buns before baking.

4 Knead the dough in a food mixer or by hand for about 7 to 10 minutes until springy and soft. Leave in a warm place for about an hour or until it has doubled in size.

5 Punch the dough down and roll out into a large rectangle shape. Mix the filling ingredients and spread across the dough, then roll tightly into a long cylinder. Cut the cylinder into slices around 2 inches (5cm) wide.

6 Preheat the oven to 425°F (220°C). To create the shape, push down firmly through the centre of each roll with an extended, flat index finger, pressing it down towards the base.

7 Brush the rolls with the remaining milk mixture and sprinkle generously with pearl sugar. Bake for about 15 minutes or until golden brown.

# WESTERN EUROPE

From the vineyards of Italy to the olive groves of Greece and lush valleys of Portugal's Douro river, cuisine from this part of the world is as diverse as the countries themselves. Historically, the Romans had a huge influence on the development of European cuisine, and preferred boiling and stewing their meat over roasting since smoke and fat were reserved for the Gods. During the Middle Ages and Renaissance, meat became the central part of the meal. European cuisine was further developed in the royal and noble courts, and in the 18th and 19th century 'cuisine classique' – a mix of aristocratic and French bourgeois cuisine – became the culinary standard in Europe. In 2010, French gastronomy was added by UNESCO to its list of the world's 'intangible cultural heritage.' There is substantial emphasis on the use of wine, sauces and dairy products in cooking, and in countries such as Austria, the Netherlands and Germany, smoking, curing, pickling and salting of foods is common.

# ITALY

From the sun-soaked vineyards of Tuscany to the Amalfi Coast, Italy offers a rich culinary journey. Each region has its own specialty – the best pizza, for example, is found in Naples, Venice is known for exquisite risotto, while the spaghetti in Rome is a must try.

This delicious clam pasta was originally considered peasant food, and has become an Italian classic. This is my favorite spaghetti dish, and so simple to make you can't get it wrong – if you can boil spaghetti you can make it *"alle vongole"*. Use fresh or frozen clams, just don't forget the white wine!

# SPAGHETTI ALLE VONGOLE

## Serves 4

1 lb (450g) fresh clams
2 tbsp olive oil
1 clove garlic
1 tsp red chilli, finely chopped
2 fl oz (60ml) white wine
1 tsp salt
Pinch pepper
1 lb (450g) dried spaghetti

TO GARNISH:
Fresh parsley

1 Bring a large pot of salted water to the boil. Add the spaghetti and cook according to the pack instructions, stirring occasionally, until just al dente.

2 To a cold saucepan, add the olive oil, garlic and chilli. Heat gently until the garlic is just golden. Add the clams and pour in the wine. Season with salt and pepper. Cover and cook over a medium heat for 3 to 4 minutes, shaking the pan occasionally.

3 Drain the pasta and transfer to a large bowl. Add the clams, including all the pan juices, and toss well. Discard any clams that are still closed. Serve immediately, garnishing with fresh parsley.

Contessa Passi taught me how to cook this dish in her beautiful Palazzo Tiepolo on the Grand Canal in Venice. Literally 'rice and peas', this classic Italian dish is much easier and less time consuming to make than a risotto. If you can't find fresh peas, use good quality frozen ones instead.

# RISI E BISI

**Serves 4**

2 ¾ pints (1.3 litres) vegetable stock
2 lb (900g) fresh peas
2 oz (60g) butter
1 onion, finely chopped
1 ¾ oz (50g) pancetta
12 ½ oz (355g) risotto rice
1 ¾ oz (50g) Parmesan cheese
2 tbsp fresh parsley, chopped

**1** Heat the vegetable stock in a large saucepan. Rinse the peas really well under running water, then add to the pot. Simmer for 2 to 3 minutes until the peas are just tender.

**2** Remove half of the peas with a slotted spoon and reserve. Blend the rest of the peas into the vegetable stock with a hand blender until smooth.

**3** Melt the butter in a large saucepan and add the onion. Cook gently on a low heat until translucent, then add the pancetta. Cook for about 5 minutes, then add the rice, stirring to make sure everything is coated in the butter.

**4** Add the vegetable stock/pea mixture and bring to the boil. Turn down to a simmer and leave to cook for about 20 minutes, stirring occasionally, until the rice is just cooked. Stir in the reserved peas and the Parmesan and season to taste. Garnish with the parsley before serving.

The very basic Pizza Margherita, named for the Queen Consort Margherita of Savoy, is my favorite of all pizzas. And also a great base for any further toppings. Extra delicious when baked in a brick pizza oven as we did in Tuscany, and as we do on board our ships, but regular ovens are just fine. Some even choose to make pizzas in a skillet!

# PIZZA MARGHERITA

## Serves 4

FOR THE PIZZA BASES:
1 x ¼ oz (7g) sachet dried
  yeast
2 tsp salt
11 fl oz (325ml) lukewarm
  water
1 lb 1 oz (500g) strong white
  bread flour
Drizzle olive oil

FOR THE TOMATO SAUCE:
Drizzle olive oil
2 cloves garlic, peeled and
  crushed
14 oz (400g) tomato passata
Salt and pepper
Fresh basil leaves, chopped

SUGGESTED TOPPINGS
(FOR 1 PIZZA):
Mozzarella, torn into small
  chunks
Parmesan, shaved or grated
Black pepper
Fresh basil leaves, torn
Drizzle extra virgin olive oil

1 Add the yeast and salt to the water and stir until dissolved. Pour this, along with the flour and oil, in to the bowl of a food processor and mix using a dough hook – first at the highest speed for 5 minutes and then at a medium speed for 8 minutes, until the dough is smooth.

2 Divide the dough into 4 roughly equal portions, pat into balls, place in a lightly oiled bowl, cover with plastic wrap and leave for about 45 minutes until the dough has doubled in size.

3 On a floured surface, roll out each dough ball until the dough is about a ¼ inch (0.5cm) thick. Stack between oiled layers of aluminum foil, cover in plastic wrap and chill for 30 minutes.

4 To make the sauce, add the olive oil to a saucepan and gently cook the garlic over a medium heat until it just begins to color. Add the passata, stir and simmer for 5 minutes. Season with salt and pepper to taste, stir in the fresh basil leaves, then take off the heat and set aside.

5 To assemble your pizza, transfer one pizza base to a lightly oiled baking sheet ready for topping. Using a tablespoon or small ladle, spread a layer of sauce on to the pizza base, making sure the sauce reaches the edge of the dough.

6 For the classic Margherita, place the mozzarella chunks evenly over the base. Scatter over the Parmesan, add a pinch of pepper and the basil leaves and finally drizzle a modest amount of extra virgin olive oil over the whole pizza. Bake for 7 to 10 minutes at 500°F (250°C) until golden and serve.

Said to originate from the northern Italian town of Treviso, this classic Venetian 'pick me up' is best left to sit for a few hours before serving to allow all the flavors to develop.

# TIRAMISU (CONTAINS RAW EGGS)

**Serves 4 – 6**

3 eggs
2 ½ oz (70g) superfine (caster) sugar
8.8 oz (250g) mascarpone
1 pack Italian sponge fingers (savoiardi)
2 tbsp Marsala wine
4 fl oz (120ml) espresso
2 tbsp cocoa
Dark chocolate, to garnish

**1** Separate the eggs, then whisk the whites until they form stiff peaks and set aside. Add the sugar to the egg yolks, then whisk until light and frothy, and add the mascarpone, little by little, whisking constantly, until completely smooth.

**2** Gently fold the whipped egg whites into the egg yolk and mascarpone mixture.

**3** In a shallow dish, add the Marsala wine to the espresso and stir. Dip the sponge fingers into the liquid just until they start to darken, but don't leave them to get soaked through.

**4** To assemble, place a layer of sponge fingers into the bottom of a serving dish, then spoon over about a third of the mascarpone mixture. Sift over a layer of cocoa. Repeat with another layer of sponge fingers and mascarpone. Finish with a dusting of cocoa.

**5** Cover and refrigerate for a few hours. Before serving, garnish with shards of dark chocolate.

## LOCAL SPECIALITY: THE BELLINI

Invented by Giuseppe Cipriani, founder of the celebrated Harry's Bar in Venice, Italy, the Bellini was originally a seasonal speciality, but quickly became a year-round favorite drink on both sides of the Atlantic.

10 cl (2 parts) Prosecco
5 cl (1 part) fresh peach purée

Pour peach purée into a chilled Champagne flute and then slowly add Prosecco. Stir gently and serve straight up, without ice.

# GREECE

With its glittering coastline and olive groves it's no surprise that seafood, olive oil and olives all feature heavily in Greek cuisine, as well as tomatoes and aubergines. Dishes can be simple – dips such as taramasalata or tzatziki, for example, or the Greek salad – or more involved, using filo pastry. And grilled skewered meat, known as *souvlaki*, is a popular classic.

Served in practically every taverna and cooked in every Greek home, this layered dish of lamb, aubergines and creamy sauce is comfort food at its best.

# TRADITIONAL MOUSSAKA

## Serves 4

Olive oil
1 lb (450g) minced lamb
1 tsp ground cinnamon
1 tsp ground ginger
1 tsp ground allspice
1 tsp cayenne pepper
1 large white onion, thinly
   sliced
1 red (bell) pepper peeled and
   chopped
2 cloves garlic, finely chopped
2 tbsp tomato paste
6 fl oz (180ml) red wine
1 tin (400g) chopped
   tomatoes in juice
2 tbsp fresh parsley
2 tbsp fresh oregano
2 tbsp honey
2 eggplants (aubergines), cut
   into ½ inch (1cm) slices

FOR THE BÉCHAMEL SAUCE:
1 pint (475ml) milk
2 oz (55g) butter
2 oz (55g) all purpose
   (plain) flour
2 eggs, beaten
Nutmeg, grated

1 Heat a tablespoon of olive oil in a large pan and add in the lamb. Sprinkle over the cinnamon, ginger, allspice and cayenne. Fry on a medium to high heat, breaking the meat up until it has completely browned.

2 Strain the meat over a bowl and reserve, discarding any liquid. Return the pan to the heat, add two tablespoons of oil and add the onion and chopped pepper. Cook until soft.

3 Add the garlic, cook for a further minute, and then add the tomato paste. Return the lamb to the pan, pour in the wine and simmer, stirring occasionally, until the wine has almost completely evaporated.

4 Add the tinned tomatoes and simmer for about 30 minutes until thickened. Stir in the parsley, oregano and honey. Season with salt and pepper, then remove from the heat.

5 To prepare the aubergine, add a generous amount of olive oil to a large, shallow pan. Season the slices on both sides with salt and pepper, and then fry in batches until soft and light brown. Transfer to paper towels to drain.

6 For the béchamel sauce, melt the butter in a medium pan. Stir in the flour and cook for a few seconds until pale and bubbling. Gradually whisk in the milk and simmer for about five minutes until thick and smooth. Season with salt, pepper and a grating of nutmeg.

7 Remove the pan from the heat and quickly stir in the beaten egg. Cover the surface of the sauce with cling wrap to prevent a skin forming.

8 To assemble the dish, preheat the oven to 350°F (175°C). Arrange half the aubergine slices in an ovenproof dish, then spoon over half the meat sauce. Top the sauce with the remaining aubergine slices, and then the remaining meat sauce. Pour the béchamel over the top of the meat sauce and spread evenly. Bake for 45 to 50 minutes until golden and bubbling.

This aromatic dish takes its name (literally 'stolen') from the 19th century when commoners, banned from owning animals, would steal lamb then completely seal it while cooking to prevent any steam or cooking smells from escaping and giving the game away!

# KLEFTIKO

**Serves 4**

4 lamb shanks
1 tbsp fresh oregano, chopped
2 tbsp olive oil
2 large white onions, roughly chopped
1 lb (450g) carrots, roughly chopped
1 tbsp fresh rosemary, chopped
2 bay leaves
1 tsp whole cloves
4 garlic cloves, chopped
2 tsp rice flour
13 ½ fl oz (400ml) red wine
1.3 pints (615ml) veal or lamb stock
2 tsp honey
2 lemons (one juiced, one sliced)

**1** Season the lamb shanks well with salt and pepper, then sprinkle over the oregano.

**2** Heat the oven to 400°F (200°C). Pour the olive oil into a large frying pan. Brown the lamb shanks all over, working in batches if necessary. Transfer to a large roasting tray.

**3** Add the chopped onions and carrots to the pan, cooking for about 10 minutes until they start to caramelize. Stir in the herbs and garlic, cooking for a further few minutes.

**4** Sprinkle over the rice flour, season well, then add the lemon juice and wine. Allow to reduce by half, then add the stock and lemon slices. Pour the mixture over the lamb shanks, then cover tightly with foil and bake in the oven for 1½ to 2 hours, until the lamb is tender.

**5** Remove the lamb from the sauce and keep warm. Place the roasting tray on the heat and allow to bubble and reduce for about 15 minutes, stirring all the time. Pass the sauce through a sieve and transfer to a saucepan. Continue to reduce until thick and glossy. Season to taste and serve.

This rich, sweet, layered pastry has been made in Greece since ancient times. The nuts used depend on the region. Popular around the Mediterranean, this pistachio version of baklava is a favorite in northern Greece.

# BAKLAVA

## Serves 8 – 10

5 oz (140g) unsalted butter
10 ½ oz (300g) whole shelled pistachio nuts
1 tsp cinnamon
10-12 sheets phyllo (filo) pastry

FOR THE SYRUP:
8 fl oz (235ml) water
9 ½ oz (280g) sugar
1 cinnamon stick
4 oz (110g) honey
1 lemon, zested

**1** Preheat the oven to 400°F (200°C), then gently melt the butter in a small saucepan.

**2** Chop the pistachio nuts finely and toss with the cinnamon, then set aside.

**3** Unroll the pastry. Make sure the layers are aligned, then cut in half, or around the size of the baking tin. Cover with a clean, wet cloth to stop the layers drying out.

**4** Brush the bottom and sides of the tin with melted butter, then place two sheets of pastry into the tin, brushing thoroughly with butter. Repeat until you have 10 sheets layered.

**5** Sprinkle with the pistachio nut mixture, then top with two more sheets of pastry, brush again with butter and sprinkle with more nuts. Repeat until you run out of pastry.

**6** Using a sharp knife, cut the baklava into diamond or square shapes around 1 x 1 ¼ inches (2 ½ x 3 cm) in size, all the way to the bottom of the pan.

**7** Bake for about 30 to 35 minutes until the baklava is golden and crisp.

**8** Meanwhile, prepare the syrup. Boil the sugar and the water without stirring for about two minutes, then add the cinnamon, honey and lemon zest. Simmer for about 20 minutes.

**9** Remove the baklava from the oven and immediately drench with the syrup. Allow to cool before serving.

# ISRAEL

The land of milk and honey has a fabulous climate yielding culinary treasures such as figs, pomegranates, oranges, lemons and grapefruits, and influences include Jewish and North African. Fresh fish, caught in the Mediterranean or the Red Sea, chicken and grilled meat are all staples.

Falafel are the ultimate Israeli street food, served stuffed into warm pita bread with a range of delicious toppings including hummus, tahini, salad and pickles. This dish works best with dried chickpeas.

# FALAFEL

## Makes 18, serves 4 – 6

8 oz (225g) dried chickpeas
1 onion, finely chopped
2 cloves garlic
2 tbsp fresh parsley, chopped
1 tsp salt
2 tsp ground cumin
1 tsp ground coriander
½ tsp dried chilli flakes
½ tsp black pepper
Vegetable oil

1 Cover the dried chickpeas in cold water and allow to soak overnight, or for at least 8 hours.

2 Drain the chickpeas and blend to a coarse paste with the rest of the ingredients (reserve a little parsley for a garnish). Cover and refrigerate until needed.

3 Heat the oil in a deep frying pan. Meanwhile, with wet hands, form the mixture into balls, using about 2 tablespoons for each ball. Once the oil is shimmering hot, fry the balls until golden brown, then drain on paper towels before serving.

The perfect accompaniment to falafel, hummus should be creamy and garlicky. If using dried chickpeas, make sure they are overcooked, very soft and cooled.

# HUMMUS

## Serves 4 – 6

14 oz (400g) tinned chickpeas, drained
2 tbsp tahini paste
4 garlic cloves
1 tsp salt
1 lemon, juiced
2 tbsp extra virgin olive oil

TO GARNISH:
Paprika

1 Place all the ingredients in a food processor, then pulse until the mixture is smooth and creamy.

2 Taste and adjust seasoning.

3 Serve in a shallow dish, garnish with a swirl of extra virgin olive oil and a sprinkle of paprika.

# TURKEY

With its roots dating back to the Ottoman Empire, Turkish cuisine is a riot of color and flavors. Specialities include köfte (balls or patties of ground beef or lamb), eggplant-based dishes, and börek, delicious savory pastries usually filled with minced meat or spinach and cheese. Street food is very popular and yoghurt accompanies pretty much everything – meat, vegetables, or simply rice or bread.

Popular all across the Middle East, these delicious, spiced meat kebabs are perfect stuffed into warm flatbreads.

# LAMB KÖFTE

**Serves 4**

2 lb (900g) minced lamb
2 red onions, finely chopped
4 garlic cloves, crushed
2 tsp dried chilli flakes
1 tsp ground cumin
2 tbsp fresh parsley
Salt and pepper
Olive oil

1 Preheat the grill, or heat a griddle pan, and soak eight bamboo skewers in water.

2 Place the minced lamb in a bowl with the chopped onion, crushed garlic, chilli flakes, cumin, parsley and a generous pinch of salt and pepper. Mix well with clean hands.

3 Split the mixture equally into 12 balls and squeeze them around the bamboo skewers to form rough sausage shapes.

4 Brush with oil and grill or griddle until golden brown all over and completely cooked through.

Don't be surprised at the amount of parsley in this classic Middle Eastern dish. It is essentially a spiced parsley salad rather than a bulgur wheat one.

# TABBOULEH

**Serves 4**

3 ½ oz (100g) bulgur wheat
13 ½ fl oz (400ml) water
1 tsp salt
1 ¾ oz (50g) fresh parsley, chopped
2 tbsp fresh mint, chopped
2 large tomatoes, chopped
4 scallions (spring onions), chopped
1 lemon, juiced
½ tsp cinnamon
½ tsp fresh cilantro (coriander), chopped
Grating of nutmeg
Extra virgin olive oil

1 Rinse the bulgur wheat in cold water until it runs clear.

2 Bring the water to the boil and add the bulgur wheat and salt, turn down to a simmer and leave for around 15 minutes. Drain, then allow to stand.

3 Meanwhile, remove the thicker stalks from all the herbs. Chop the parsley, mint, tomatoes and scallions. Add to the bulgur wheat along with the lemon juice and spices. Season to taste and add a drizzle of extra virgin olive oil.

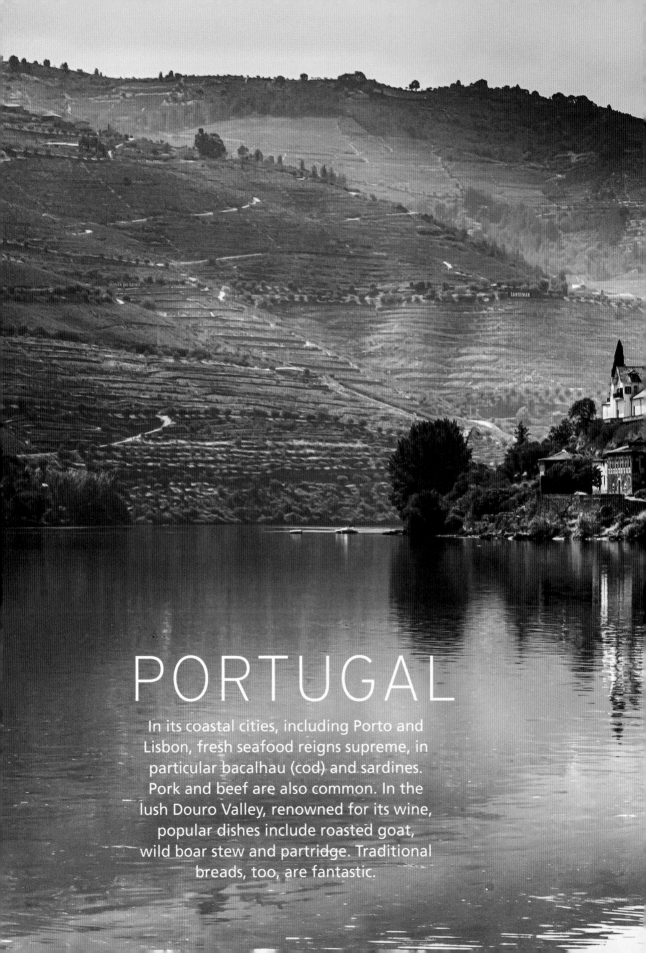

# PORTUGAL

In its coastal cities, including Porto and Lisbon, fresh seafood reigns supreme, in particular bacalhau (cod) and sardines. Pork and beef are also common. In the lush Douro Valley, renowned for its wine, popular dishes include roasted goat, wild boar stew and partridge. Traditional breads, too, are fantastic.

Bacalhau is one of Portugal's most famous dishes, and they say there are as many recipes for Bacalhau as there are days in the year. Today they even create alchemy versions of the dish – which is difficult to recreate at home, without a Michelin chef like Rui Paula to guide you. What all the variants have in common are that they are all made with Norwegian stockfish (dried and salted cod), which has bonded the countries and cultures of Portugal and Norway for centuries.

# BACALHAU À BRÁS

## Serves 4

1 lb (450g) dried salted cod
1 lb (450g) waxy potatoes
Olive oil
1 large white onion, halved,
   then thinly sliced
2 bay leaves
4 cloves garlic, crushed
2 tbsp fresh parsley, chopped
4 large eggs
1 oz (30g) black olives, pitted

TO GARNISH:
Dash of Tabasco
Lemon wedges

1 Cover the cod in cold water and allow to soak for approximately 48 hours, changing the water frequently.

2 Place the cod in a large pot and cover with water again. Boil for about 15 minutes, then drain. Allow to cool, then flake and set aside.

3 Peel the potatoes and cut into matchsticks. Add 1 to 2 tablespoons of olive oil to a non-stick pan and fry the potatoes in batches. Keep the cooked matchsticks warm in a low oven.

4 Add a further tablespoon of olive oil to the pan and add the bay leaves. Cook for 2 to 3 minutes, then add the garlic and onions to the pan. Sauté until translucent. Discard the bay leaves, then add in the parsley and the flaked cod.

5 Mix the eggs with a fork, then add to the pan. Keep stirring until the eggs are scrambled. Combine the fries with the cod mixture, then stir in the olives. Season to taste and finish with a dash of Tabasco. Garnish with lemon wedges.

Often served for special occasions, this creamy baked custard dessert, topped with a layer of caramel, can be cooked in individual tarts or in one large flan. This recipe is so simple I learnt to cook it from Francesco in Porto without understanding a word of what he was saying!

# CARAMEL FLAN

## Serves 8 – 10

FOR THE CARAMEL:
3 ½ oz (100g) sugar
2 tbsp water

FOR THE CUSTARD:
5 oz (140g) sugar
6 eggs
1 tsp vanilla extract
1 pint (475ml) whipping cream
10 fl oz (300ml) milk

1 Preheat the oven to 300°F (150°C). Place the sugar and water in a saucepan over a medium heat. Cook without stirring, swirling the pan occasionally, until the caramel turns a deep golden brown.

2 Lightly oil individual metal molds or one baking tin, then carefully pour in the caramel, allowing it to run right to the edges. Take care as the liquid will be extremely hot.

3 Make the custard by whisking the eggs and sugar together in a bowl until light and frothy. Meanwhile, heat the cream and milk together in a saucepan over a low heat until steaming hot, but not boiling. Drizzle a little into the custard, whisking continuously, then slowly add the rest of the milk, whisking all the time.

4 Place the metal molds or baking tin into a large roasting pan. Strain the custard into a jug, then gently pour over the caramel. Place the roasting pan in the oven, then carefully add boiling water around the molds or tin until it reaches halfway up the sides. Bake for about an hour or until just set.

5 Allow to rest until the dessert reaches room temperature, then carefully turn out onto a serving plate.

Found all around Portugal, these delicious little custard tarts are traditionally served dusted with sugar and cinnamon. It's impossible to eat just one.

# PASTÉIS DE NATA

## Makes roughly 12

8 ½ fl oz (250ml) milk
1 lemon, zest only
1 cinnamon stick
3 ½ oz (100g) superfine (caster) sugar
2 tbsp all purpose (plain) flour
2 ½ fl oz (75ml) water
3 large eggs, yolks only
11 ¼ oz (320g) all-butter puff pastry

**1** Preheat the oven to 475°F (245°C). Gently heat the milk with 2 to 3 strips of lemon zest and the cinnamon stick to a simmer, then remove the lemon and cinnamon.

**2** Mix the flour with a little of the milk to a smooth paste, then stir in the rest of the milk. Return to the heat, whisking constantly for a few minutes until thick.

**3** Place the sugar and water in a saucepan, stirring until the sugar has dissolved. Bring to a boil and allow to boil for 3 minutes, then whisk into the milk mixture.

**4** Place the egg yolks in a bowl and slowly add the milk mixture, whisking constantly. Transfer to a jug and allow to cool slightly.

**5** Lightly butter all the holes in a 12-hole muffin tin. Roll the pastry out into a rough rectangle, then roll each rectangle up from the bottom to the top. Cut each roll into 12 discs. Place one disc flat into the base of each muffin hole, then, with wet thumbs, gently press out until the pastry comes about half way up each hole.

**6** Pour the custard into the pastry cases, then bake for about 15 minutes, until set and caramelized. Sprinkle with sugar and cinnamon, then serve while still warm.

# SPAIN

More so perhaps than any other European cuisine, Spanish gastronomy is influenced by the culture, society, geography and climate of its different regions. In Andalucia, home to Seville and the flamenco, Serrano ham and Iberico ham are both popular. Valencia is the place to try paella, while Barcelona is known for its Catalan cuisine, with seafood, tomatoes, red peppers, eggplant, mushrooms and artichokes featuring.

Paella recipes vary hugely, but this Catalan-style paella contains monkfish, which holds together well during the cooking process, as well as tender squid, and peas, which add sweetness. Spanish paella is always made in a paellera, a large, flat pan with two handles. Native paella eaters all know: the best bit is the crusty bit at the bottom, and is know as the *"socarrat"*, as I learned at my favorite tapas place in Barcelona, just off Las Ramblas.

# PAELLA CATALUNYA

## Serves 4

1 pinch saffron threads
2 pints (950ml) fish
   stock
2 tbsp olive oil
7 oz (200g) monkfish, cut
   into bite-size pieces
2 cloves garlic, crushed
1 large Spanish onion,
   chopped
1 tsp paprika
2 red bell peppers, chopped
   and deseeded
9 oz (250g) paella rice
4 large fresh tomatoes,
   deseeded and chopped
5 oz (140g) frozen peas
1 lb (450g) squid,
   cleaned and sliced
9 oz (250g) mussels, scrubbed,
   beards removed
1 tsp salt
1 tsp pepper

TO GARNISH:
4 tbsp fresh parsley, chopped

**1** Place the saffron threads into a large, wide, heavy-based pan over a medium heat and stir constantly until they just begin to give off their aroma. Add the stock and bring to the boil. Transfer to a saucepan, cover and set aside to infuse.

**2** Return the pan to the heat and add one tablespoon of oil. Add the monkfish pieces and quickly fry on all sides until lightly browned. Remove the fish and set aside.

**3** Add another tablespoon of oil to the pan. Add the garlic, onion and paprika and cook over a moderate heat for two minutes, stirring occasionally. Stir in the red peppers and continue cooking until all the vegetables are soft but not brown.

**4** Add the rice and stir well, ensuring all the grains are well coated. Bring the saffron-infused stock to simmering point and add half of it to the rice. Stir, and then bring to the boil. Lower the heat and simmer for five minutes or until almost all the liquid is absorbed.

**5** Add the remaining stock, then stir in the tomatoes, peas and reserved monkfish pieces. Add the squid and simmer for five minutes. Arrange the mussels around the dish, pushing them into the rice. Simmer for a further 15 minutes or until the rice is tender and all the liquid has been absorbed. Season with salt and pepper to taste. Remove the pan from the heat, cover with foil and leave to stand for five minutes. Discard any mussels that have not opened. Garnish generously with parsley before serving.

These rich meatballs, served in a spicy tomato sauce, often feature on traditional Spanish tapas menus. For a main course, serve with crisp patatas fritas.

# ALBÓNDIGAS CON TOMATE

## Serves 4

9 oz (250g) minced beef
9 oz (250g) minced pork
1 Spanish onion, chopped
2 cloves garlic, crushed
3 tbsp breadcrumbs
2 tbsp Cheddar cheese, grated
2 tsp smoked sweet paprika
1 tbsp fresh oregano leaves
1 egg
Salt and pepper

FOR THE SAUCE:
2 tbsp olive oil
1 Spanish onion, chopped
2 cloves garlic, crushed
1 red chilli, deseeded and
  finely chopped
1 tbsp fresh basil, chopped
6 large tomatoes, chopped
1 tbsp balsamic vinegar
Salt and pepper
2 tbsp fresh parsley, chopped

FOR THE GARLIC CROUTONS:
1 small baguette
2 oz (55g) butter
2 cloves garlic, crushed
1 tbsp fresh parsley, chopped

**1** Preheat the oven to 350°F (175°C). To make the meatballs, combine the beef, pork, onion, garlic, breadcrumbs, Cheddar cheese, paprika and oregano in a bowl together with the egg. Season generously.

**2** With wet hands, shape the mixture into meatballs, weighing around 1 ¾ oz (50g) each. Refrigerate for half an hour.

**3** Meanwhile, make the garlic croutons. Melt the butter in a saucepan and add the crushed garlic and chopped parsley. Cut the bread into cubes and toss the cubes in the butter mixture. Spread out on a baking tray and bake for around 20 minutes or until crisp and golden. Keep warm until needed.

**4** Next, heat the oil in a large frying pan and cook the meatballs in batches, turning frequently, until they have browned all over. Transfer to a baking tray and place in the oven for 10 minutes.

**5** To make the sauce, add the onion to the pan and cook until just soft and translucent. Add the garlic, chilli and basil and cook for 30 seconds, then add the chopped tomatoes and balsamic vinegar. Bring to the boil and season well with salt and plenty of black pepper.

**6** Remove the meatballs from the oven and add them to the tomato sauce. Cover and simmer for 10 minutes. Serve with the garlic croutons.

# LOCAL SPECIALITY: SHERRY

Made from white grapes that are grown near the town of Jerez, in southern Spain, sherry is a fortified wine; its name is an Anglicization of the town's name. Under Spanish law, all wine labeled as sherry must legally come from the Sherry Triangle, an area between Jerez, Sanlúcar and El Puerto. Sherries can be drunk any time of the day but are typically enjoyed as an aperitif or after dinner.

Often eaten for breakfast, these delicious treats should be covered in sugar and cinnamon as soon as they come out of the hot oil. Smooth hazelnut paste makes the chocolate sauce extra special.

# CHURROS

## Serves 4

8 fl oz (235ml) milk
2 oz (55g) butter
4 tbsp sugar
Pinch salt
9 oz (250g) all-purpose (plain) flour
3 eggs
Vegetable oil for deep frying

### FOR THE CINNAMON SUGAR:
2 ½ oz (70g) granulated sugar
2 tsp ground cinnamon

### FOR THE CHOCOLATE SAUCE:
8 ½ fl oz (250ml) whipping cream
9 oz (250g) dark chocolate, chopped
2 tbsp hazelnut (praline) paste

**1** Place the milk, butter, sugar and salt in a saucepan and bring to a simmer.

**2** Add the flour to the pan and mix well to combine, cooking gently and stirring until the mixture forms a soft dough. Take the pan off the heat and beat in the eggs.

**3** Heat the oil in a deep fat fryer (or deep saucepan) to 375°F (190°C). Test the temperature with a small amount of dough.

**4** Spoon the mixture into a piping bag with a star-shaped nozzle and pipe the mixture carefully into the hot oil, snipping each churro off with a pair of scissors. Fry until golden brown, then drain on paper towels. Toss the churros in the cinnamon sugar while still hot.

**5** For the chocolate sauce, heat the cream in a small saucepan and then pour over the chopped chocolate, stirring continuously until the sauce is smooth. Stir in the hazelnut paste and serve immediately with the churros.

# FRANCE

As you might expect, cheese and wine play a major part in all French cuisine, but each region has its own speciality. In Normandy dishes made with seafood, and apples are abundant; Provence and the Côte d'Azur are renowned for fresh vegetables, fruits and herbs; and in Burgundy, specialities include pike, perch, snails, game, redcurrants and blackcurrants.

Originally cooked by fishermen using unwanted fish from their catch, this traditional Provençal fish stew is served with a creamy, saffron-scented rouille.

# BOUILLABAISSE TOULONNAISE

**Serves 4**

Olive oil
4 ½ oz (125g) fennel, sliced
2 red onions, chopped
1 tsp sea salt
1 tbsp tarragon, chopped
½ tsp black pepper
Fish heads, bones and offcuts
2.2 lb (1kg) tomatoes,
    roughly chopped
2 tbsp tomato purée
1 pinch saffron threads
1 lemon, juiced
2 tbsp butter

FOR THE ROUILLE:
3 egg yolks
Salt and pepper
½ lemon, juiced
Pinch saffron
Pinch cayenne pepper
6 ¾ fl oz (200ml) olive oil
2 cloves garlic, crushed

7 oz (200g) salmon
7 oz (200g) pollock
7 oz (200g) monkfish
1 lb (450g) mussels, scrubbed,
    beards removed

1 To make the broth, heat 4 tablespoons of olive oil in a large pan over a medium heat. Add the fennel and cook for 3 to 4 minutes without it coloring, then add the red onion, sea salt, tarragon and black pepper.

2 Add the fish bones and offcuts and the tomatoes, then cover with water. Bring to a simmer, skimming off any residue that rises to the surface. Add the tomato purée and saffron and bring back to a simmer. Cook for about 1 ½ hours, or until it has reduced by about a third.

3 Sieve the broth, pressing down the contents of the sieve with a ladle to extract as much liquid as possible, then add the lemon juice and whisk in the butter. Check the seasoning, then cool and refrigerate until needed.

4 To make the rouille, whisk the egg yolks with the seasoning, lemon juice, saffron and cayenne pepper. Slowly add the oil in a thin stream, whisking continuously, then stir in the garlic. Add a little warm water if it's too thick. Set aside until needed.

5 Bring the reserved broth up to a simmer, then add all the fish. Poach until just tender, adding the firmest fillets first, then remove and place on a serving platter. Ladle over the broth. Serve with the rouille on the side and some garlic croutons.

This hearty French dish traditionally contains a whole bottle of Burgundy. For the bouquet garni, tie sprigs of rosemary and thyme, parsley stems and bay leaves tightly together with kitchen string.

# BOEUF BOURGUIGNON

**Serves 4**

Olive oil
3 ½ oz (100g) bacon lardons
1 large white onion, sliced
2 tbsp all purpose (plain) flour
Salt and pepper
1.3 lb (600g) lean stewing
   steak
1 bottle (75 cl) Burgundy or
   other good red wine
1 garlic clove, crushed
1 bouquet garni
6 oz (170g) button
   mushrooms
6 oz (170g) whole baby
   onions

1 Preheat the oven to 325°F (160°C). Heat two tablespoons of olive oil in a heavy casserole dish and fry the bacon lardons until golden brown. Remove from the pan and reserve. Repeat with the sliced onion, frying until soft.

2 Mix the flour together with a generous amount of salt and pepper and toss the steak well in the seasoned flour. Shake off the excess, then fry in batches until well browned, adding more oil if needed.

3 Deglaze the pan with a glassful of red wine. Allow the liquid to bubble and scrape all the caramelized bits from the bottom of the pan. Return the bacon, onions and beef to the pan with the garlic and bouquet garni. Pour in the rest of the red wine. If the meat isn't completely covered, add a little beef stock or water.

4 Put on a lid and place the casserole in the oven. Cook for about 2 ½ hours.

5 About 30 minutes before the end of the cooking time, fry the baby onions and mushrooms until golden and add to the beef. Remove the bouquet garni before serving.

The list of ingredients may look daunting, but this classic French recipe is actually very simple to follow and makes an impressive dinner party dish. Ask your butcher for the duck liver, or substitute a chicken liver.

# POITRINE DE CANARD BRAISÉE À LA ROUENNAISE

## Serves 4

1 tsp juniper berries
1 tsp caraway seeds
1 tbsp allspice
Salt and pepper
3.3 fl oz (100ml) Cognac
1 medium duck

FOR THE SAUCE:
2 tbsp butter
8 oz (225g) shallots, finely
   chopped
1 tsp fresh thyme
1 bottle (75 cl) red wine
1 tsp corn starch (cornflour)
1 pint (475ml) veal or chicken
   stock

FOR THE DAUPHINOISE
POTATOES:
1.4 lb (650g) potatoes
6 ¾ fl oz (200ml) milk
6 fl oz (175ml) heavy (double)
   cream
1 clove garlic, crushed
1 bay leaf
1 or 2 sprigs thyme
7 oz (200g) Gruyère cheese
Nutmeg, freshly ground
Salt and pepper

1 To prepare the duck, first grind the juniper berries, caraway seeds, allspice, 1 teaspoon of salt and a few grinds of pepper with a pestle and mortar. Mix the spice mix with the Cognac then rub the mixture generously inside the duck. Leave to stand for at least 3 hours.

2 Preheat the oven to 350°F (175°C), then tip the duck up and carefully strain any remaining liquid, reserving it for the sauce.

3 Place the duck on a wire rack above a roasting tray and roast for 20 minutes per 1 lb (500g) plus an extra 20 minutes. Remove from the oven, cover and rest in a warm place while you make the sauce.

4 Melt the butter in a pan, then add the shallots and cook them slowly until translucent. Add the thyme and the reserved Cognac mixture, then reduce. Add the red wine, then reduce again until glossy. Finally, add the stock and reduce again. Remove a couple of tablespoons of the sauce, stir into the cornflour until smooth, then return this to the sauce. Before serving, add the chopped duck liver.

5 To make the dauphinoise potatoes, peel and thinly slice the potatoes. Bring the milk and the cream to the boil with the garlic, bay leaf and sprigs of thyme. Butter a baking tin, then arrange a layer of the sliced potatoes across the base. Season, then sprinkle with grated cheese. Repeat until all the potatoes have been used. Finally, carefully pour over the milk and cream mixture, grate over some nutmeg and bake at 320°F (160°C) for about 35 to 45 minutes until golden brown.

Make sure that the pan you use for cooking this delicious French dessert is ovenproof. Once cooked, it's best left until just warm before serving.

# TARTE TATIN

**Serves 6**

3 ½ oz (100g) superfine
   (caster) sugar
2 oz (55g) butter
6 dessert apples
2 tbsp butter
11.2 oz (320g) all-butter
   puff pastry

1 Preheat the oven to 350°F (175°C). Heat the sugar and butter over a medium heat until it turns a deep golden brown. Don't allow the caramel to burn.

2 Peel and halve the apples, scooping out the seeds with a spoon. Place all the apples in the caramel and cook, moving them around in the caramel, for about 10 minutes. Next, in a 9 inch (23cm) diameter oven proof dish or pan, arrange the apple halves, rounded side down. Fill in any gaps with cut apples and dot with small pieces of butter.

3 Roll the pastry out into a circle, slightly larger than the pan and about 0.2 inch (5mm) thick. Place the disc of pastry over the caramelized apples, tucking the edges in all around the dish. Brush with melted butter.

4 Bake for around 30 to 40 minutes, or until the pastry is golden brown and the caramel is starting to ooze from the tart. Leave to cool for an hour before serving.

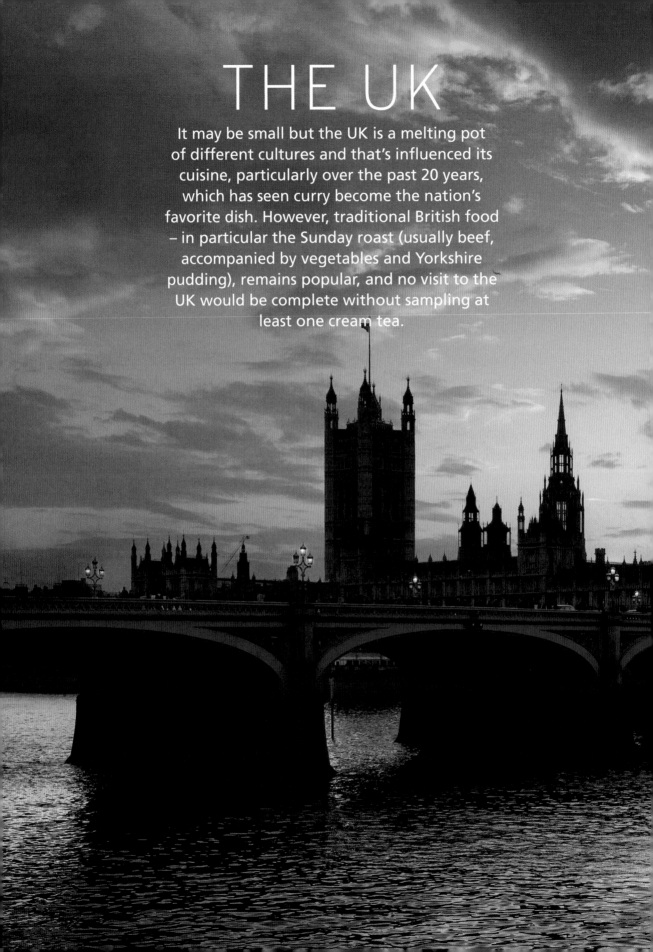

# THE UK

It may be small but the UK is a melting pot of different cultures and that's influenced its cuisine, particularly over the past 20 years, which has seen curry become the nation's favorite dish. However, traditional British food – in particular the Sunday roast (usually beef, accompanied by vegetables and Yorkshire pudding), remains popular, and no visit to the UK would be complete without sampling at least one cream tea.

My favorite dish from boarding school, shepherd's pie always brings back fond memories of my childhood in England. As the name suggests, traditional shepherd's pie is made with minced or leftover roast lamb. If made with beef, it becomes a cottage pie. Both are delicious!

# SHEPHERD'S PIE

## Serves 4 – 6

2 tbsp olive oil
1 large onion, peeled and
   chopped
2 lb (900g) minced lamb
1 tbsp fresh thyme
1 tbsp Worcestershire sauce
2 tbsp all purpose
   (plain) flour
1 pint (475ml) veal or lamb
   stock
1 ½ lb (680g) floury potatoes
2 oz (55g) butter
2 ½ fl oz (75ml) milk

1 Heat the oil in a large, heavy based saucepan, then add the chopped onion and fry until translucent. Add the meat and fry until it has completely browned, then stir in the thyme and Worcestershire sauce.

2 Sprinkle over the flour and stir into the mince, then stir in the stock. Bring to the boil, turn down the heat and simmer for about 30 minutes.

3 Meanwhile, peel and chop the potatoes. Bring to the boil in a large pan of salted water, turn down the heat and cover, simmering until very tender.

4 Preheat the oven to 350°F (175°C). Drain and mash the potatoes, then stir in the butter and milk. Season with salt and pepper to taste. Transfer the mince into an ovenproof serving dish, then top with the mashed potatoes. Bake in the oven for about 20 minutes or until bubbling and golden.

This comforting old English recipe, full of spice and dried fruit, was originally created to use up stale bread, but has become a classic 'nursery' dish.

# BREAD AND BUTTER PUDDING

## Serves 4 – 6

1 day-old loaf of white bread,
cut into 8-10 thick slices
3 ½ oz (100g) butter
3 oz (85g) sultanas
2 tsp cinnamon
12 ½ fl oz (370ml) milk
2 ½ fl oz (75ml) heavy
(double) cream
2 large eggs
2 tbsp granulated sugar

TO GARNISH:
Fresh nutmeg
Brown sugar

**1** Preheat the oven to 350°F (175°C), then butter a pie dish generously. Cut the crusts off the bread and butter each slice, then cut each slice diagonally in half.

**2** Arrange the bread slices in the dish, buttered side up, overlapping as much as possible until the bottom of the dish is covered. Next, sprinkle over half the sultanas and 1 teaspoon of the cinnamon.

**3** Repeat with a second layer, sprinkling over the remaining sultanas and cinnamon.

**4** To make the custard, heat the milk and cream together in a pan until just at simmering point. In a mixing bowl, whisk together the eggs and sugar until light and creamy.

**5** Gently whisk the warmed milk into the egg mixture, whisking thoroughly, then pour over the bread layers. Garnish with a grating of nutmeg and a scattering of brown sugar.

**6** Bake in the oven for 30 to 40 minutes until the custard has set and the pudding is golden brown.

How you eat your cream tea will depend on where you're eating it (it's cream first, then jam in Devon, but jam first, then cream in Cornwall), and there's serious disagreement about whether the cream should be double or clotted. What's not in doubt is that it should always be served in the afternoon, with a pot of tea.

# CREAM TEA

**Makes 8 – 10 scones**

8 oz (225g) all purpose
   (plain) flour
Pinch of salt
2 tsp baking powder
2 oz (55g) butter
2 tbsp superfine (caster) sugar
5 fl oz (150ml) milk

**1** Preheat the oven to 425°F (220°C). Lightly butter a baking sheet and set aside.

**2** Mix together the flour, salt and baking powder. Cut the butter into cubes and, using just your fingertips, rub gently into the flour until it resembles breadcrumbs.

**3** Stir in the sugar. Add the milk little by little and continue stirring until the mixture comes together into a soft dough.

**4** Flour the work surface and then roll the dough out to about ¾ inch (2cm) thick. Use a medium fluted cutter to cut out the scones and place them on the buttered baking sheet.

**5** Brush the scones with a little milk, then bake for 12 to 15 minutes until risen and golden brown. Split the scones and serve with strawberry jam, cream and a pot of tea.

"Afternoon Tea", a book in the Finse of Dogton Abbey series, written by the Countess of Carnarvon of Highclere Castle, with a child-friendly recipe on how to bake scones

# THE NETHERLANDS

Splendid windmill-studded tulip fields,
colorful Amsterdam and a rich culture make
the Netherlands an idyllic destination for
sightseeing. Simple and straightforward,
Dutch cuisine has been shaped by its fishing
and farming, with many vegetables and lots
of fish; bread and cheese are also popular,
as of course are pancakes.

These crisp meatballs, filled with a creamy ragout, were originally created to use up leftovers, but are now more often found as a tasty accompaniment to a Dutch beer.

# BITTERBALLEN

### Serves 4 – 6

1 small onion, finely chopped
1 ¾ oz (50g) butter
2 tbsp all purpose (plain) flour
10 fl oz (300ml) beef stock or
   leftover gravy
1 tbsp fresh parsley, chopped
14 oz (400g) cooked beef,
   shredded
Salt and pepper
Nutmeg, grated
Vegetable oil, for frying
2 oz (55g) all purpose
   (plain) flour
2 eggs, beaten
3 oz (85g) breadcrumbs

1 To make the roux, fry the onion in the butter until soft and translucent, then stir in the flour. Continue to cook until the mixture is pale and bubbling, then slowly whisk in the beef stock to make a very thick sauce.

2 Stir in the parsley and the cooked beef and season with the salt and pepper. Add a grating of nutmeg, then set aside to cool.

3 To make the bitterballen, take a tablespoon of the cold beef mixture and, with floured hands, quickly roll it into a ball, then coat with the beaten egg, and then finally with the breadcrumbs. Heat the oil until shimmering hot, then fry in batches until golden brown. Serve with mustard.

This traditional Dutch soup is comforting and creamy.
Serve with green grapes and caramelized walnuts.

# CREAMY CHEESE SOUP

**Serves 4**

4 tbsp oil
1 tbsp butter
1 large white onion
2-3 slices smoked streaky
  bacon, chopped
1 cauliflower, broken into
  florets
6 oz (170g) potatoes, peeled
  and chopped
4 large carrots, peeled and
  chopped
1 tbsp fresh thyme
1 pint (475ml) chicken stock
5 oz (140g) Gouda cheese,
  grated
4 tbsp heavy (double) cream
Salt and pepper, to taste

FOR THE CARAMELIZED
WALNUTS:
2 ½ oz (70g) walnuts, roasted
1 oz (30g) sugar
1 tbsp water

TO SERVE:
14 oz (400g) green grapes,
  peeled, seeded, and
  quartered

1 Add the oil and butter to a heavy frying pan and fry the onion and bacon until sizzling. Add in the cauliflower, potatoes and carrots and continue to cook on a low heat until softened.

2 Add in the fresh thyme, then stir in the chicken stock. Bring to a boil, then simmer until all the vegetables are tender. Add the cheese and cream, then blend with a stick blender until very smooth. Season to taste.

3 To make the caramelized walnuts, heat the sugar and water until it forms a thick syrup, then coat the walnuts with the syrup and allow to cool on a non-stick baking sheet.

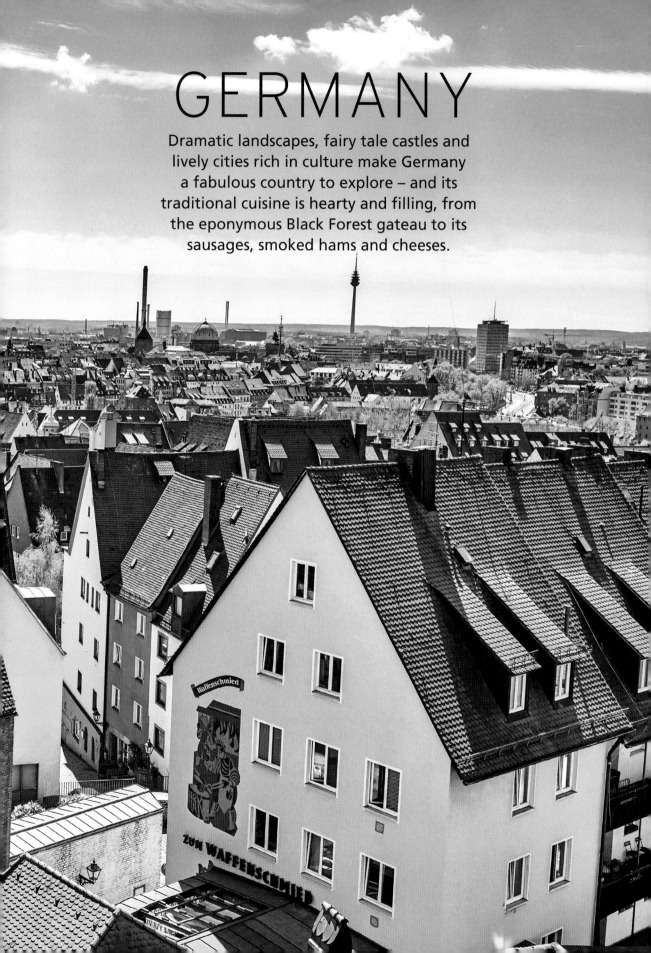

# GERMANY

Dramatic landscapes, fairy tale castles and lively cities rich in culture make Germany a fabulous country to explore – and its traditional cuisine is hearty and filling, from the eponymous Black Forest gateau to its sausages, smoked hams and cheeses.

Literally meaning 'sour roast', this German version of a pot roast is marinated for 24 hours, giving a deliciously tender result that's full of flavor. Serve with crisp potato dumplings.

# BEEF SAUERBRATEN

## Serves 4 – 6

2 lb (900g) beef roasting joint
Salt and pepper
4 tbsp olive oil
6 ¾ fl oz (200ml) water
5 fl oz (150ml) apple cider
   vinegar
11 fl oz (325ml) red wine
   vinegar
½ tsp juniper berries
½ tsp cloves
2 bay leaves
6 ¾ fl oz (200ml) cold water

FOR THE ONION MIXTURE:
1 tbsp (15g) butter
2 large white onions, chopped
2 carrots, chopped
2 celery stalks, chopped
2 cloves garlic, crushed
2 pints (950ml) veal or chicken
   stock
2 tbsp sugar
4 fl oz (120ml) balsamic
   vinegar
2 tbsp (30g) butter

FOR THE POTATO
DUMPLINGS:
Vegetable oil, for frying
1 lb (450g) floury potatoes
Nutmeg, grated
1 tbsp sour cream,
1 tbsp (15g) butter
2 egg yolks
8 oz (225g) all purpose
   (plain) flour
2 eggs, beaten
8 oz (225g) panko
   breadcrumbs

1 Season the beef well on all sides with salt and pepper. Heat the oil in a heavy based pan and brown the joint on all sides. Remove the meat and reserve.

2 To make the marinade, pour the water, apple cider vinegar and red wine vinegar into the hot pan and bring to a simmer, scraping any caramelized bits from the bottom of the pan. Add in the juniper berries, cloves and bay leaves, and season with salt and black pepper.

3 Remove the pan from the heat and add the cold water, then pour the mixture over the meat, cover and chill quickly. Marinate in the refrigerator for 24 hours.

4 Melt the butter in a large casserole dish over a medium heat. Add the onion, carrot and celery and cook for 10 minutes until the vegetables have softened. Add the garlic and cook for a further minute.

5 Remove the beef from the marinade and set to one side. Pour the marinade into the vegetables, stir in the stock and sugar, then finally place the beef on top. Bring to a simmer, then reduce the heat and cover, cooking for about 3 to 4 hours until the meat is completely tender.

6 Remove the meat on to a platter. Discard the juniper berries, cloves and bay leaves. Spoon the cooked onion mixture over the top of the meat, reserving the excess cooking liquid in the pan. Place the pan back on the heat and stir in the balsamic vinegar. Reduce the sauce for about 20 minutes, skimming off any fat. Finally, strain, season to taste and whisk in a little cold butter for an extra glossy sauce.

7 To make the potato dumplings, preheat a deep fat fryer to 375°F (190°C). Boil the potatoes in plenty of salted water until tender, then mash and add seasoning, a grating of nutmeg, the sour cream, butter and egg yolks. Beat until smooth.

8 With floured hands, shape the potato mixture into balls. Roll each ball in flour, patting off any excess, then roll in the beaten egg and finally the breadcrumbs. Fry until golden and serve.

You might be surprised to see that a whole bottle of wine goes into this fresh vegetable soup, but the rich buttery Riesling complements the celeriac perfectly. Garnish with delicate puff pastry twists.

# RIESLING SOUP

**Serves 4**

4 ½ oz (125g) butter
3 large white onions, chopped
7 oz (200g) celeriac, chopped
2 bay leaves
1 bottle (75 cl) German
   Riesling
2 ½ pints (1.2 liters) chicken
   stock
8 ½ fl oz (250ml) heavy
   (double) cream
Salt and pepper

FOR THE PASTRY TWISTS:
2 oz (55g) all-butter
   puff pastry
1 egg yolk
Pinch paprika

1 Melt the butter in a heavy pan over a low heat. Add the onion, celeriac and bay leaves. Gently fry until the vegetables are soft and translucent. Be careful not to add any color.

2 Deglaze the pan with the white wine, then add the chicken stock. Allow to simmer until the vegetables are completely soft and the liquid has reduced by half. Blitz with a hand blender until smooth, then pour in the cream and season well.

3 To make the puff pastry twists, preheat the oven to 425°F (220°C). Brush the pastry with egg yolk, then sprinkle with paprika. Cut the pastry into ¾ inch (2cm) strips. Gently twist the strips, then lay on a non-stick baking tray. Bake for 8 to 10 minutes or until golden brown.

This fermented German preserve is so easy to make at home and the results are delicious. Make sure everything is scrupulously clean before you start.

# SAUERKRAUT

1 large kilner jar, sterilized
1 large, firm green cabbage
1 ½ tbsp good quality sea salt
   or kosher salt

1 Core and thinly slice the cabbage, then place in a large mixing bowl. Sprinkle over the salt and combine well using your hands, squeezing the salt and cabbage together for about 10 minutes.

2 Transfer the cabbage and all the liquid to the jar, pressing it down well. Use a clean weight to keep the cabbage under the surface of the liquid. Do not replace the lid, but cover the top of the jar with a clean cloth or muslin.

3 Allow the cabbage to ferment at room temperature, and out of direct sunlight, for a week to 10 days, pressing it down frequently so that it remains under the surface of the liquid.

4 Keep tasting the sauerkraut and when it is done to your liking, remove the weight, secure the lid and store in the refrigerator, where it will keep for at least two to three months.

The Black Forest's most famous dessert, Schwarzwälder Kirschtorte, should traditionally contain kirsch, a clear spirit made from cherries. This recipe uses jars of cherries in kirsch, but if you can't find them, soak canned or fresh cherries in kirsch or brandy overnight before using.

# BLACK FOREST GATEAU

## Serves 6 – 8

6 oz (170g) butter, at room temperature

6 oz (170g) superfine (caster) sugar

6 large eggs, whisked

5 oz (140g) all purpose (plain) flour

2 tsp baking powder

2 tbsp cocoa powder

1 ½ lb (680g) black cherries in kirsch syrup

1.6 pints (750ml) heavy (double) cream

7 oz (200g) bar of dark chocolate

1 To make the cakes, preheat the oven to 350°F (180°C) and grease and line two large (9 inch/23cm) springform cake tins.

2 Beat the butter and sugar together until pale and creamy, and then slowly add about half the eggs.

3 Sift together the flour, baking powder and cocoa and add about half to the butter and sugar mixture, then add the remaining eggs and finally the remaining flour mixture.

4 Split the mixture evenly between the two cake tins and level the tops. Bake for about 30 minutes or until the cakes are springy to the touch. Set aside to cool.

5 Drain the cherries, reserving the liquid, and chop into small pieces, reserving 12 for decoration.

6 Cut each of the cooled cakes in half horizontally. Whip the cream to the stiff peak stage.

7 To assemble, start with one of the cake halves. Drizzle generously with kirsch syrup, then spread over a thick layer of whipped cream. Scatter over a third of the chopped cherries. Repeat again with the next two layers. For the final layer, drizzle with kirsch syrup, then pile on the remaining cream.

8 For the chocolate shards, brace the chocolate against you, flat side up, and carefully bring the blade of a sharp knife towards you, shaving the chocolate into curls and shards. Shower the top of the cake with the chocolate shards. Finally, decorate with the remaining whole cherries.

# AUSTRIA

From its magnificent capital, Vienna, the Danube River and the music of Mozart, Strauss, Schubert and Haydn, Austria is utterly enchanting. With so many woods, game is a traditional element of Austrian cuisine, along with seasonal vegetables and fruits like pumpkin. Wiener Schnitzel, exquisite pastries and desserts are all highlights of Austrian cuisine – plus of course the deliciously indulgent Sachertorte.

These very thin, crisp breaded veal steaks are the national dish of Austria. I learned from Michelin starred chef Tony Morwald how fast and simple this dish named in honor of Vienna really is to make. Serve with potatoes, ideally boiled in water and butter, and garnish with parsley and a lemon wedge.

# WIENER SCHNITZEL

## Serves 4

4 veal escalopes, approx.
   4 ½ oz (125g) per person
4 ½ oz (125g) all purpose
   (plain) flour
Salt and pepper
2 eggs, beaten
8 oz (225g) breadcrumbs
9 oz (255g) butter
1 lb (450g) potatoes, cooked,
   peeled and sliced
2 oz (55g) butter
Small bunch fresh parsley
1 lemon

1 Place the veal escalopes on a board and gently tap with a rolling pin until thin and even. Breadcrumb the veal escalopes by preparing three plates: one with the flour, seasoned generously, one with the beaten eggs and one with the breadcrumbs. Dip the escalopes first in the flour, brushing off the excess, then in the egg wash and then into the breadcrumbs, pressing them firmly onto the meat.

2 Heat the butter in a heavy based pan and skim off any residue. Deep fry the escalopes in the butter, basting frequently, until golden brown, then drain on kitchen towel. Keep warm.

3 Serve the escalopes with boiled potatoes dressed in butter and chopped parsley, and a lemon wedge.

## LOCAL SPECIALITY: SCHNAPPS

From the traditional taverns of southern Germany to Viennese restaurants and Swiss ski lodges, schnapps has been warming the souls of those that drink it for centuries. A strong, clear alcoholic drink resembling gin, it is often flavored with fruit, such as apples, pears or cherries. The word 'schnapps' derives from the Old Norse verb *'snappen'*, meaning to snatch or gulp, an indication as to how the drink should be taken: neat, ice cold and swiftly. Keep your bottle of schnapps in the freezer (the high level of alcohol will prevent it from freezing solid) and serve small quantities in shot, sherry or, better still, authentic schnapps glasses.

Originally created by chef Franz Sacher in 1832, this most famous of Viennese desserts should be served with a decadent pile of whipped cream. Visit Hotel Sacher in Vienna to sample the original Sachertorte.

# SACHERTORTE

## Serves 8 – 10

5 oz (140g) butter, softened
3 ½ oz (100g) confectioners' (icing) sugar, sieved
8 eggs, separated
5 oz (140g) bittersweet (dark) chocolate
2 ¾ oz (80g) all purpose (plain) flour
3 ½ oz (100g) sugar
2 tbsp apricot jam

FOR THE GLAZE:
8 oz (225g) bittersweet (dark) chocolate
2 tbsp butter

1 Preheat oven to 375°F (190°C) and grease and line a 9 inch (23cm) cake tin. Cream together the butter and icing sugar, then mix in the egg yolks, one at a time, until very creamy.

2 Melt the chocolate in a heatproof bowl placed over a saucepan of simmering water. Do not allow the bowl to touch the water. Gradually add the melted chocolate into the creamed mixture, then fold in the flour.

3 In a separate bowl, beat the egg whites until they form soft peaks then gradually fold in the sugar. Combine this mixture with the chocolate mixture.

4 Pour the cake mixture into the prepared tin and bake for about 50 minutes to an hour until springy to the touch. Remove from the pan and cool on a wire rack. Heat the apricot jam and smooth over the entire torte, including the sides.

5 For the glaze, melt the chocolate and butter together in a bain-marie until smooth and glossy. Pour over the cake, making sure it's completely covered, and allow to cool before serving.

# EASTERN EUROPE

Eastern European cuisine is closely connected to the political, social and economic revival of its countries following long periods of historical upheaval. Strongly influenced by its climate, which can be particularly harsh during the winter, recipes from this region tend to be substantial and comforting. Meat, root vegetables and smoky flavors feature heavily, alongside more intricate gourmet offerings such as appetizers and tortes. Pancakes, breads and berries are also important. Spices such as paprika, herbs and sour cream are all used throughout the region. Because it's surrounded by so many lakes and mountains, fish and seafood are plentiful in Eastern Europe, and in the Black Sea area, the native juniper wood is used for smoking hams and sausages.

# CZECH REPUBLIC

Located at the heart of Central Europe,
this small nation boasts spectacular
cultural treasures and a rich tapestry of
natural wonders, such as the stunning
cliffs along the Elbe River. Influenced by its
surrounding countries, potato soup, roast
pork and sauerkraut, strudel, dumplings
and cabbage all feature heavily in its
cuisine. Bread is traditionally sourdough
baked from rye and wheat. Stews and
dumplings are also popular.

Nothing in the world smells better than freshly baked bread! This easy recipe, which can be made by hand or in a food processor, recreates the traditional taste and texture of Czech rye bread recipe without the need for a sourdough starter. Best served piping hot with a dollop of butter!

# RYE BREAD

## Makes 2 loaves

14 oz (400g) strong white
  bread flour
11 ½ oz (325g) rye flour
2 x ¼ oz (7g) packs of fast
  action dried yeast
1 tbsp salt
4 tbsp sugar
2 tsp caraway seeds
1 tbsp fennel seeds
3 tbsp lard (vegetable
  shortening)
1 pint (475ml) water

1 In a large mixing bowl, combine the flours with the yeast, salt, sugar and seeds. Mix well.

2 In a saucepan, gently heat the water and lard until the lard has melted. Slowly pour the hot liquid into the flour mixture, stirring all the time just until the dough comes together. You may not need to add all the liquid, but the dough should be quite sticky.

3 Knead the dough for about 5 minutes, either in a food processor with a dough hook or by hand (although it is easier in a food processor as the dough benefits from being really moist). Cover with a clean cloth and allow to rise somewhere warm for about an hour.

4 Punch the dough down, divide in two and shape into round loaves. Place on a non-stick baking sheet and allow to rise for a further 30 minutes. Preheat the oven to 375°F (190°C) and bake for 35 to 40 minutes until golden brown and hollow when tapped.

# CROATIA

Formerly part of Yugoslavia, Croatia's location
on the Adriatic Sea means that seafood is
in abundance here, as are game and veal.
Charcuterie is part of Croatian tradition.
Manistra na pome – pasta with tomato sauce –
is a staple; gnocchi is also a must-try.

The beautiful bay of Mali Ston just north of Dubrovnik is famous for producing the most incredible oysters, and pulling oysters fresh from the turquoise blue waters is one of my fondest travel memories. The oysters are absolutely delicious eaten with nothing more than a squeeze of lemon, but locally you'll also find them grilled with a simple, seasoned butter. Filled with proteins, iron, omega 3 calcium, zinc and vitamin C, you can eat oysters with a good conscience!

# GRILLED OYSTERS

### Serves 4

16 fresh oysters, shucked
2 cloves garlic, crushed
Freshly ground black pepper
2 oz (55g) softened butter

TO GARNISH:
Lemon wedges

1 Preheat the grill to its hottest setting. Mash the garlic and pepper into the softened butter.

2 Arrange the oysters on a baking sheet, adding a teaspoon of seasoned butter to each one. Grill for 5 to 6 minutes or until the edges of the oysters start to puff up. Serve simply garnished with a wedge of lemon.

This traditional Croatian seafood dish gets its unusual color from squid ink. Sachets of ink are widely available from supermarkets and fishmongers.

# BLACK RISOTTO

## Serves 4

1 lb (450g) cherry tomatoes
2 tbsp olive oil
2 cloves garlic, crushed
1 lb (450g) squid, prepared
  and sliced
2 tbsp olive oil
2 cloves garlic, finely chopped
2 ½ pints (1.2 liters) fish stock
2 tbsp butter
1 small onion, chopped
12 ½ oz (355g) Carnaroli
  risotto rice
5 fl oz (150ml) white wine
Salt and pepper
1 x 4g sachet squid ink

1 Prepare the cherry tomatoes. Blanch briefly in boiling water, then remove with a slotted spoon, peel and chop.

2 In a frying pan, heat the olive oil, then add the crushed garlic and the squid. Sauté really fast and remove from the pan as soon as the squid starts to curl. Reserve and keep warm.

3 In the same pan, add a further 2 tablespoons of olive oil and the chopped garlic. Briefly fry the garlic until golden and then add all of the chopped cherry tomatoes. Cook gently until reduced and thickened, then add in the squid. Season with salt and pepper to taste, then keep warm.

4 For the risotto, heat the fish stock in a saucepan, then in a heavy based pan melt the butter, add the onion and cook for 5 minutes until soft without coloring the onion. Add the rice and stir well, coating in the oil, then add the white wine and cook the rice until all the wine has been absorbed, stirring all the time.

5 Begin to add the warm fish stock, a ladle at a time, stirring the risotto constantly and never allowing it to dry out. Add the squid ink to the risotto and keep stirring, then keep adding the stock until the rice is just tender and the risotto is slightly runny. This should take about 15 minutes.

6 Serve the risotto and top with the squid in tomato sauce.

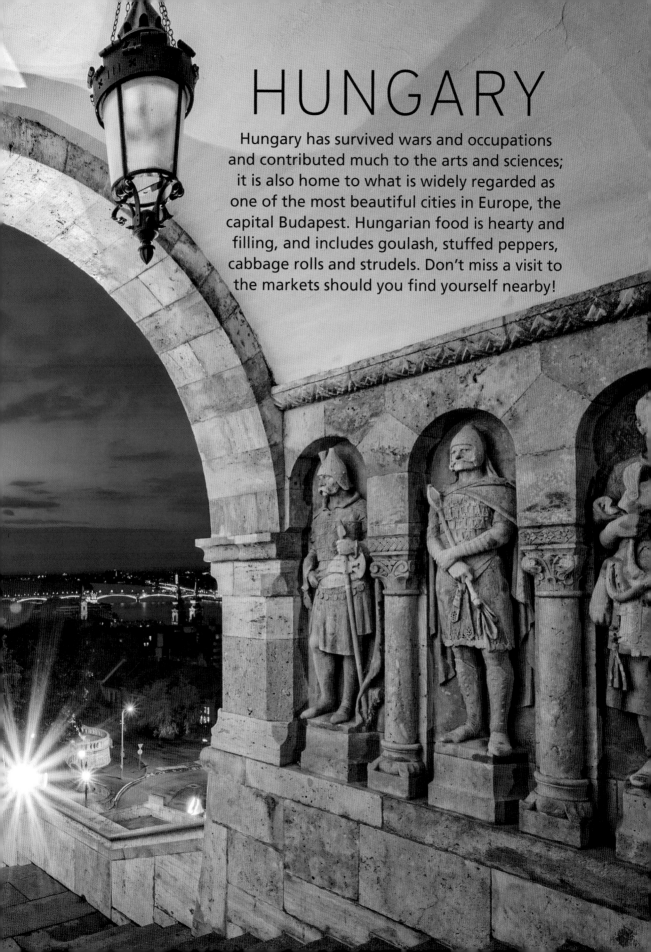

# HUNGARY

Hungary has survived wars and occupations and contributed much to the arts and sciences; it is also home to what is widely regarded as one of the most beautiful cities in Europe, the capital Budapest. Hungarian food is hearty and filling, and includes goulash, stuffed peppers, cabbage rolls and strudels. Don't miss a visit to the markets should you find yourself nearby!

Hungarian goulash is a thick, hearty soup spiced with sweet paprika. Serve with a dollop of sour cream.

# GOULASH

## Serves 4 – 6

2 tbsp oil
1 large onion, finely chopped
2 lb (900g) lean stewing steak
3 carrots, chopped
3 celery stalks, chopped
2 cloves garlic, sliced
1 green bell pepper, deseeded
    and chopped
2 large tomatoes, skinned
    and chopped
3 pints (1.4 liters) beef stock
2 tsp paprika
1 lemon
Salt and pepper
3 large white potatoes,
    peeled and chopped
Sour cream

**1** In a large pot, heat the oil, then fry the onion for about five minutes until softened. Add the beef and fry, stirring constantly, until completely browned (add a little more oil if necessary).

**2** Add the carrots, celery, garlic and chopped pepper, then fry for a further 5 minutes.

**3** Stir in the tomato, stock and paprika. Season generously with salt and pepper and add a good squeeze of lemon juice. Turn the heat up and bring to a boil, then lower the heat, cover and simmer for about 1 hour and 30 minutes, until the meat is completely tender. Add the potatoes about 20 minutes before the end of cooking time. Serve in bowls and garnish with a large spoonful of sour cream.

Whereas goulash is a thick soup, pörkölt is a much more substantial stew. The meat used differs according to region, but it is often made with beef, pork or chicken, and served with pasta. Don't miss a visit to the markets should you find yourself nearby!

# CHICKEN PÖRKÖLT

**Serves 4**

4 chicken breasts, cubed, or
  1 whole chicken, cut into
  pieces
3 tbsp olive oil
1 onion, chopped
1 green bell pepper, deseeded
  and chopped
3 cloves garlic, sliced
3 tbsp paprika
1 pinch dried chilli flakes
14 oz (400g) tinned chopped
  tomatoes in their juice
1 pint (475ml) chicken stock
Salt and pepper

1 In a heavy based casserole dish, heat the oil, then fry the onion and green pepper for about five minutes until softened. Add the garlic, paprika and chilli flakes, and stir well.

2 Pour in the chopped tomatoes and stock. Season generously with salt and pepper, then stir in the meat. Turn the heat up and bring to a boil, then lower the heat, cover and simmer for about an hour, until the meat is completely tender.

3 Serve immediately with pasta or gnocchi.

## LOCAL SPECIALITY: PÁLINKA

It would be impossible to visit Budapest or anywhere else in Hungary without having a glass (or two) of the traditional fruit brandy known as Pálinka. Invented in the Middle Ages, Pálinka is made from fruits grown on the Great Hungarian Plain. The most common Pálinkas are made from apricots, pears and plums, although cherries, apples, quince, mulberries and chestnuts are also used.

The first records of Pálinka date back to the 14th century, when it became the *aqua vitae* of the wife of the King Charles of Hungary. This spirit was probably a brandy blended with rosemary and had medicinal properties, as both the King and the Queen suffered from arthritis.

Today, the Hungarians mark every important occasion – birthdays, weddings, funerals – with a shot of Pálinka.

Pálinkás jó reggelt!, is a traditional Hungarian greeting meaning 'Good morning with pálinka!'

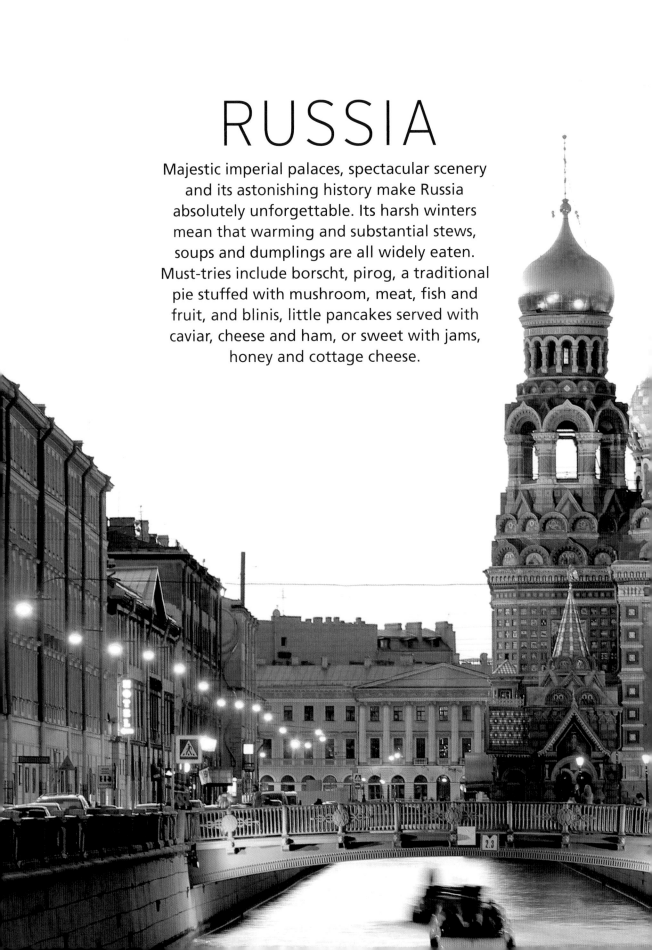

# RUSSIA

Majestic imperial palaces, spectacular scenery and its astonishing history make Russia absolutely unforgettable. Its harsh winters mean that warming and substantial stews, soups and dumplings are all widely eaten. Must-tries include borscht, pirog, a traditional pie stuffed with mushroom, meat, fish and fruit, and blinis, little pancakes served with caviar, cheese and ham, or sweet with jams, honey and cottage cheese.

Russian dishes tend to be warming and hearty and stroganoff, a staple since the mid-19th century, is no exception. Serve with extra sour cream, like a real Russian.

# BEEF STROGANOFF

## Serves 4

1 ½ lb (680g) stewing beef
Salt and pepper
4 oz (115g) butter
Small bunch scallions
   (spring onions), chopped
2 tbsp all purpose
   (plain) flour
9 ½ fl oz (280ml) beef stock
2 tsp Dijon mustard
6 oz (170g) sliced mushrooms
5 fl oz (150ml) sour cream,
   plus extra for garnish
5 fl oz (150ml) white wine

**1** Trim any excess fat or gristle from the meat. Season generously with salt and pepper.

**2** Heat the butter in a large pan and add the beef, frying until browned on all sides, then turn the heat down and push the beef to one side of the pan. Add the spring onions and cook slowly for around 5 minutes until softened.

**3** Sprinkle the flour over the meat and onions and stir everything together, making sure the flour is completely absorbed, then pour in the beef stock and bring to the boil, stirring constantly.

**4** Lower the heat and stir in the mustard, then cover and simmer for an hour or until the meat is tender. 10 minutes before serving, stir in the mushrooms, sour cream and white wine. Season to taste and serve.

Russian babushkas pride themselves on passing down home cooking skills to the next generations. My adopted babushka Nadya who lives in Uglich along the Volga river makes the world's best soups, and her borscht is otherworldly! Originally Ukrainian, this vibrant soup is like most soups in Russia traditionally topped with sour cream and chopped dill. Served warm in winter, it is a satiating classic; served cool in summer it is a refreshing treat.

# BORSCHT

## Serves 4

3 pints (1.4 liters) chicken
stock
3 potatoes, peeled and
chopped
½ a green cabbage, very
finely shredded
3 tbsp olive oil
3 medium beetroots, peeled
and chopped
1 red onion, finely chopped
3 tbsp tomato purée
2 bay leaves
1 lemon
3 tbsp chopped dill

TO GARNISH:
2 oz (55g) sour cream

1 Heat the stock in a large pot and add the potatoes. Bring to a simmer and cook for about 15 to 20 minutes until tender. Add the sliced cabbage and cook for another five minutes.

2 Meanwhile, heat the oil in a frying pan and gently sauté the beetroot and red onion until soft, then stir in the tomato purée. Transfer the contents of the pan into the stock pot and stir through, adding the bay leaves, a good squeeze of lemon juice and two tablespoons of the chopped dill. Season well with salt and pepper to taste and simmer for a further 15 minutes. Serve garnished with sour cream and the remaining dill.

# ASIA

Asia is home to many cultures, all with their own distinctive cuisine. Even rice comes in many different varieties, popular in different regions – jasmine rice, for example, is found across southeast Asia including Vietnam and Cambodia, while long-grain rice is widely eaten in China. There are some ingredients however which are common to many cultures in eastern and southeast Asia, including ginger, garlic, chillies, soy and tofu. Chinese cuisine originated over 4,000 years ago in what is known as the Eight Great Traditions, including the native cooking styles of Hunan and Sichuan provinces, known for their bold flavors. The Chinese also invented the wok and stir-fry technique. Vietnamese recipes use a wide range of herbs, including lemongrass, mint and cilantro, while Cambodian cuisine includes tropical fruits; both cuisines have French influences dating back to when they were colonies.

# CHINA

Cosmopolitan Shanghai, imperial Beijing
and the legendary Yangtze River –
China is one of the most remarkable
countries in the world, and its cuisine is
equally extraordinary. From sheng jian
(pan-fried meat dumplings) to crisp-skinned
Peking duck, China offers an incredible
array of food.

Using the sweet and sour flavors originating from the province of Hunan, this Chinese favorite is a lighter alternative to the deep fried pork found in many Western versions.

# SWEET AND SOUR PORK

## Serves 4

FOR THE MARINADE:
1 tsp soy sauce
½ tsp cornstarch (cornflour)
1 tsp Chinese rice wine

Oil for frying
1 lb (450g) pork loin, cubed
1 clove garlic, finely chopped
1 tsp fresh ginger, grated
1 red bell pepper, deseeded
   and chopped
1 green bell pepper, deseeded
   and chopped
1 bunch scallions
   (spring onions), white part
   only, chopped
3 ½ oz (100g) fresh or tinned
   pineapple, chopped
1 tbsp tomato purée
1 tbsp plum sauce
1 tbsp Worcestershire sauce
1 tbsp Chinese rice wine
   vinegar
1 tbsp oyster sauce
1 tbsp honey
2 tbsp pineapple juice or
   water

1 Mix together the marinade ingredients and stir in the pork. Allow to marinate for half an hour, mixing occasionally.

2 Heat the oil in a large, heavy based frying pan and fry the pork until golden brown, then remove and set aside.

3 Add the garlic and ginger to the pan and fry briefly. Add the peppers and scallions and cook until softened, then add the pineapple pieces and finally the pork.

4 In a bowl, mix together the tomato purée, plum sauce, Worcestershire sauce, rice wine vinegar, oyster sauce, honey and pineapple juice, then pour into the pan. Cook just until the sauce thickens then serve immediately with rice or noodles.

These Chinese dumplings can be filled with either meat or vegetables and are a family favorite, traditionally served during Chinese New Year.

# POT STICKERS

## Makes 20 dumplings

9 oz (250g) minced pork or
  chicken
2 scallions (spring onions)
  finely chopped
1 oz (30g) tinned bamboo
  shoots, finely chopped
1 tsp fresh ginger, grated
1 tbsp cornstarch (cornflour)
Pinch of white pepper
2 tsp soy sauce
1 pack round Chinese
  dumpling wrappers
2 tbsp vegetable oil
5 fl oz (150ml) water

FOR THE DIPPING SAUCE:
6 tbsp soy sauce
4 tbsp Chinese black vinegar
  or balsamic vinegar
2 tbsp sesame oil
2 tbsp chilli garlic sauce

**1** In a bowl, mix the pork with the scallions, bamboo shoots and ginger. Sprinkle over the cornstarch and pepper and mix well together, then stir in the soy sauce.

**2** Place a tablespoon of the pork mixture in the center of each dumpling wrapper, brush the edges with water, fold in half and press against the edges to seal, pressing lightly down to form a flat bottom.

**3** Heat a large, heavy based frying pan and add a tablespoon of oil. Add half of the pot stickers and cook for 3 to 5 minutes until the bottoms are golden brown. Add half the water, cover and reduce the heat, steaming for another 3 to 5 minutes until all the water is absorbed. Transfer the cooked dumplings to a warm plate, and then repeat the frying and steaming process with the remaining pot stickers.

**4** Mix all the dipping sauce ingredients together and serve immediately with the hot pot stickers.

This crisp, aromatic roast duck is originally from Beijing and surprisingly simple to make. Serve with the classic accompaniments of pancakes, crisp vegetable strips and plum sauce.

# PEKING DUCK

## Serves 4

2 ½ lb (1.2kg) duck
Sea salt
Black pepper
Five spice powder

Chinese pancakes, steamed
Plum sauce
Cucumber, cut into sticks
Scallions (spring onions),
   sliced lengthways

**1** Preheat the oven to 325°F (160°C). Place the duck on a wire rack in the sink and pour over a kettle of boiling water, then rub the duck all over, inside and out, with sea salt. Sprinkle pepper and five spice powder generously all over the duck.

**2** Place the duck on a rack over a roasting tin and roast for two hours, emptying the tray occasionally as it fills with fat. Allow to rest for 10 to 15 minutes before serving.

**3** To serve the duck, shred the meat and serve with steamed Chinese pancakes, the scallions, cucumber and some plum or hoisin sauce.

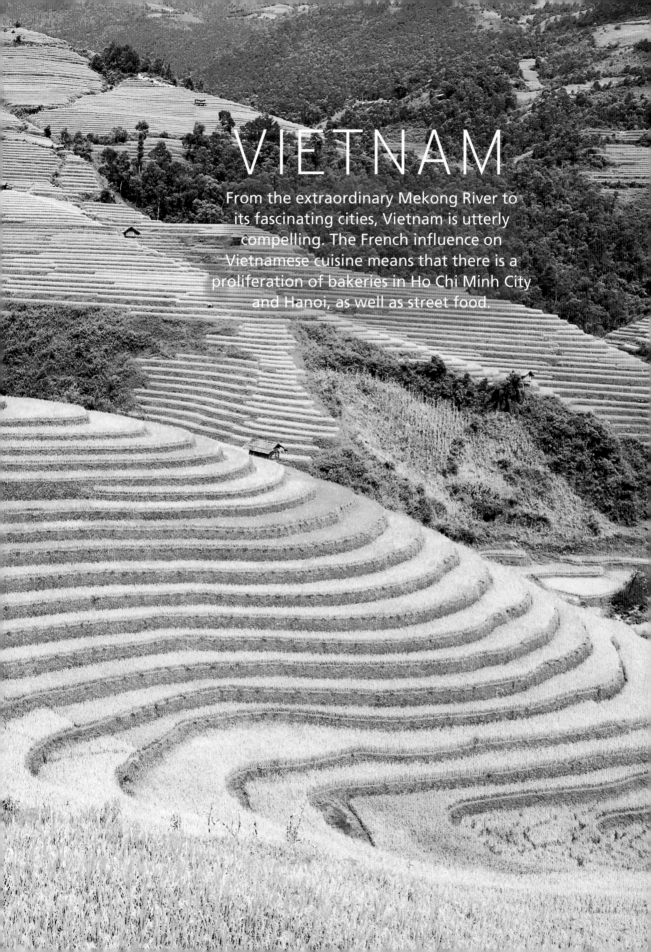

# VIETNAM

From the extraordinary Mekong River to its fascinating cities, Vietnam is utterly compelling. The French influence on Vietnamese cuisine means that there is a proliferation of bakeries in Ho Chi Minh City and Hanoi, as well as street food.

Originating in northern Vietnam in the early 20th century, pho remains a popular street food and is considered Vietnam's national dish. The aromatic broth served with this traditional recipe can take several hours to cook. This quicker version uses ready-made beef stock infused with classic flavors.

# BEEF PHO

## Serves 4

3 pints (1.4 liters) veal or beef
   stock
1 onion, chopped
2 whole star anise
½ cinnamon stick
1 clove
½ tsp whole peppercorns
1 thick slice fresh ginger
2 tsp sugar
1 tsp salt
1 tsp fish sauce
1 pack flat rice noodles
9 oz (250g) sirloin steak

TO GARNISH:
Sriracha (Vietnamese hot chili
   sauce)
Hoisin sauce
1 onion, thinly sliced
Fresh cilantro (coriander),
   chopped
Bean sprouts
Sweet Thai basil leaves
Thinly sliced scallions
   (spring onions)
Limes, quartered

1 Make the aromatic broth by heating the stock in a saucepan and adding in the onion, star anise, cinnamon stick, clove, peppercorns, ginger, sugar, salt and fish sauce. Allow to simmer for at least 30 minutes, then strain and return to the pan, discarding the spices.

2 Meanwhile, cook the rice noodles until soft, according to packet instructions.

3 Slice the steak as thinly as possible, then place some noodles into each bowl, and top with a few raw beef slices. Ladle the boiling broth over the beef and noodles and serve with the garnishes and sauces.

Vietnam is famous for its bánh mì. These baguettes with a Southeast Asian twist are filled with all sorts of delicious fillings. Create your own favorite – the trick is to combine lots of different flavors and textures.

# BÁNH MÌ

**Serves 4**

FOR THE PICKLED CARROT:

2-3 carrots, grated
1 tsp salt
3 ½ oz (100g) sugar
4 fl oz (120ml) white vinegar
4 fl oz (120ml) water

4 small baguettes, or 1 large
    cut into 4
Mayonnaise
Soy sauce
Chicken liver pâté
Cooked pork, beef or chicken
Sliced ham
Sliced cucumber
Cilantro (coriander)
1 chilli, thinly sliced

**1** For the quick pickled carrot, grate the carrots, or cut into very thin matchsticks, then combine the rest of the ingredients and pour over the carrots. Stir well, then cover and leave for at least an hour (will keep for a couple of weeks refrigerated).

**2** Slice the baguette lengthwise. Mix the mayonnaise with the soy sauce and spread over the inside of the baguette.

**3** Continue layering your chosen contents: chicken liver pâté, the cooked meat, ham, cucumber, cilantro, slices of chilli and the pickled carrot. Finish with extra cilantro and serve.

## LOCAL SPECIALITY: THE GRAHAM GREENE

It was at the Metropole Hotel, in Vietnam's capital Hanoi, in 1951 that English author Graham Greene first ordered the drink that would become his eponymous cocktail. His favored tipple – essentially a dry martini with an added splash of crème de cassis – perfectly suited the hotel's elegant French colonial-style façade. Try experimenting with your quantities; more vermouth makes a 'wetter' drink; more gin dries it out. Those who prefer a slightly sweeter or fruitier drink should up their measure of cassis.

MAKES ONE SERVING:

2 fl oz (60ml) gin
¾ fl oz (20ml) Noilly Prat (dry white
    vermouth)
A dash of crème de cassis (blackcurrant
    flavored liqueur)

In a cocktail shaker, combine the ingredients over plenty of ice cubes and shake vigorously for 30 seconds. Pour into a chilled martini glass, straining the ice as you go, and serve immediately, without a garnish.

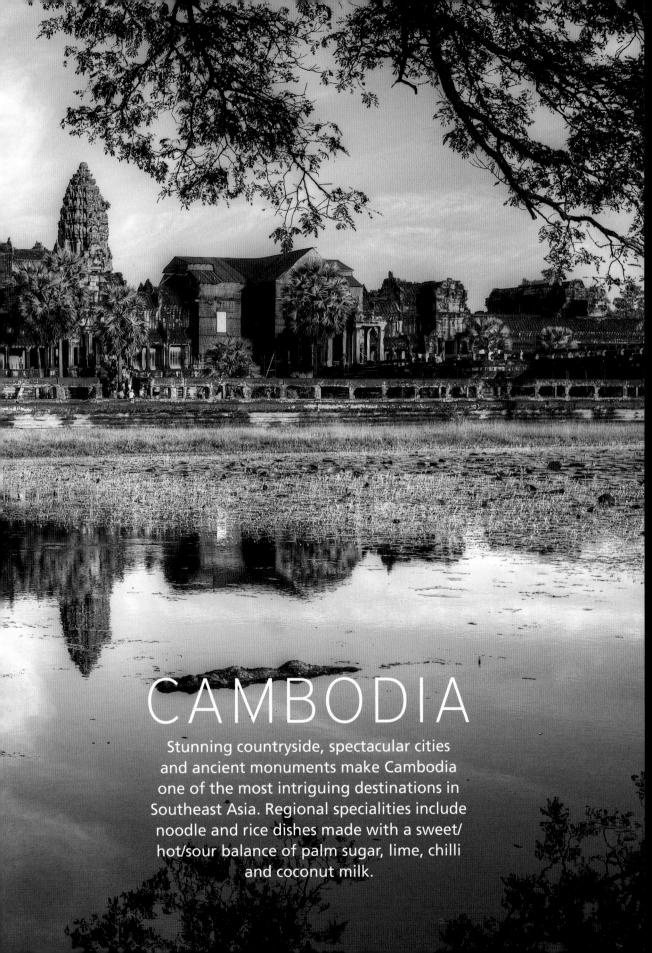

# CAMBODIA

Stunning countryside, spectacular cities
and ancient monuments make Cambodia
one of the most intriguing destinations in
Southeast Asia. Regional specialities include
noodle and rice dishes made with a sweet/
hot/sour balance of palm sugar, lime, chilli
and coconut milk.

The red chicken curry typical to Cambodia is much less fiery and more aromatic than its Thai counterparts.

# KHMER RED CHICKEN CURRY

## Serves 4

1 lemongrass stalk, chopped
1 tbsp turmeric
2 tbsp fresh ginger, grated
2 kaffir lime leaves
6 cloves of garlic, chopped
1 red chilli, deseeded and
   chopped
1 shallot, peeled and chopped
2 tbsp oil
1 lb (450g) chicken, either
   breast or leg/thigh meat
2 tbsp sugar
1 tbsp fish sauce
2 sweet potatoes, peeled and
   chopped
1 carrot, chopped
1 potato, chopped
4 star anise
7 oz (200g) tinned coconut
   milk
Pinch salt
1 lime

1 To make the aromatic paste, pound the lemongrass, turmeric, ginger, lime leaves, garlic, chilli and shallot together to make a smooth paste.

2 Heat the oil in a heavy based saucepan or wok and fry the curry paste for 1 to 2 minutes. Add the chicken, then the sugar and fish sauce. Fry until the chicken is opaque, and then add the vegetables.

3 Next, pour over the coconut milk, and add a pinch of salt, the star anise and a splash of water. Simmer until the chicken is cooked through and the vegetables are tender. Before serving, add a squeeze of lime and serve with steamed rice or crisp slices of baguette.

One of Cambodia's best-loved breakfast dishes is bai sach chrouk (pork with rice). The pork is tenderized in a coconut milk marinade before being grilled over charcoal and served with rice, pickles and sometimes a cup of clear chicken broth.

# BAI SACH CHROUK

**Serves 4**

14 oz (400g) lean pork loin, thinly sliced

FOR THE MARINADE:
3 garlic cloves, crushed
2 tbsp soy sauce
2 oz (55g) grated palm sugar, or use light brown sugar
7 oz (200g) tinned coconut milk
2 tbsp fish sauce
1 lime, juiced

FOR THE PICKLES:
2-3 carrots, grated
Half cucumber, cut into thin strips
Handful of fresh cilantro (coriander) leaves
1 tsp salt
3 ½ oz (100g) sugar
4 fl oz (120ml) white vinegar
4 fl oz (120ml) water

**1** First, make the marinade by combining all the ingredients together. Add the pork, cover and allow to marinate for a few hours, ideally overnight.

**2** To make the pickles, grate the carrots and cut the cucumber into thin strips, then combine the rest of the ingredients and pour over the vegetables. Add in the cilantro, stir well, then cover and leave for at least an hour (will keep for a couple of weeks refrigerated).

**3** Remove the pork from the marinade and either grill or barbecue until well caramelized and completely cooked through. Serve with steamed white rice and the pickled vegetables.

## LOCAL SPECIALITY: RICE WINE

Alcoholic beverages fermented from rice were once exclusive to East and Southeast Asian countries, but over the centuries knowledge of the distillation process reached South Asia through trade. Today, rice wine is popular throughout Asian cuisine and is used in much the same way as grape wines are used in European cuisine. Each country has its own variation of rice wine: saké from Japan; mijiu, a clear, sweet Chinese liqueur, and sombai, a Cambodian rice wine infused with spices, while the Vietnamese drink their rice wine though thin bamboo tubes.

# NORTH AMERICA
# & THE CARIBBEAN

Early Native Americans used a variety of cooking methods which were blended with European techniques to form the basis of modern American cuisine. The early colonists farmed meat and had similar cuisine to Britain, although the pioneers had to make use of whatever food was available to them. The first American cookbook was actually published in 1796. Multiple ethnic and regional approaches have also had a huge influence on American cuisine. Caribbean cuisine is also a melange of different influences, including the Carib, Arawak and Taino ancient tribes, and Spanish, French, African, Indian and Chinese. Barbecue was actually invented by the Arawaks, who used to cook meat on a wood fire so that it imbibed the smoky flavors, while 'soul food' also originated with the tribes; and jerk seasoning was created by escaped African slaves who cooked wild boar without smoke to keep their hiding places a secret.

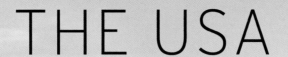

# THE USA

North American cuisine varies tremendously from region to region, drawing on ethnic influences as well as local produce and climate. In Alaska and the Pacific Northwest, salmon is a staple; the Deep South has its roots in French and Creole cuisine; New England is renowned for its seafood: a personal favorite of mine is steamers and melted butter best eaten on the rocks with good company at sunset; California is known for its fresh fruit and salads; and New York for its pastrami sandwiches as well as cuisine from all over the world.

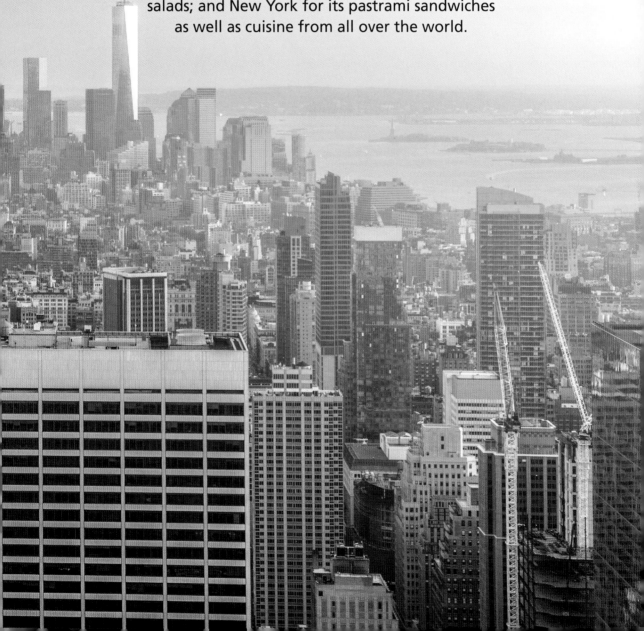

Although ingredients differ across New England, the classic Boston chowder contains cream, clams and potatoes. The New York variant is tomato based and a very different flavor and texture. Should you have been so lucky to spend a summer on Cape Cod or the Maine coast, let this clam chowder bring back those memories of sun, sand and sea.

# BOSTON/NEW ENGLAND CLAM CHOWDER

## Serves 4

1 oz (30g) butter
6 slices streaky bacon, chopped
2 onions, chopped
3 tbsp flour
1 pint (475ml) chicken stock
1 ¼ lb (565g) tinned clams in brine
2 bay leaves
4 potatoes, peeled and chopped
8 fl oz (235ml) heavy (double) cream
Salt and pepper

TO GARNISH:
2 slices streaky bacon, chopped

1 Heat the butter in a large saucepan. Add the bacon, fry for a couple of minutes, then add the onions and fry for a further five minutes or until just softened.

2 Sprinkle over the flour and stir to combine, then pour over the stock, stirring well. Strain the clams and add the clam liquid into the pot.

3 Add the bay leaves, potatoes and cream and bring to a simmer, stirring regularly, then reduce and cover for about 20 minutes until the potatoes are tender.

4 Meanwhile, fry the remaining two slices of bacon until golden and crispy, then reserve and keep warm.

5 Finally, remove the bay leaves, add the clams and season to taste. Cook just until the clams are heated through, then serve. Garnish with the crispy bacon.

New York's 21 Club is credited with serving the original New York gourmet burger back in 1950. Since then, a whole new trend for artisan burgers has emerged, but the original New York gourmet burger, served with Cheddar cheese, tomato, pickles and grilled onions, still takes some beating.

# GOURMET BURGER

**Serves 4**

1.65 lb (750g) minced beef
   containing about 20% fat
1 shallot, very finely chopped
Salt and pepper
2 beefsteak tomatoes, sliced
2 large white onions, sliced
8 slices streaky bacon
4 slices Cheddar cheese
4 brioche buns

1 Place the beef into a bowl and add the chopped shallot. Season very generously with salt and pepper, then mix well and divide into four large burgers, pressing your thumb down gently into the centre of each burger. Cover and refrigerate until needed.

2 Preheat a skillet or griddle pan and brush lightly with oil. Place the burgers onto the skillet and leave to cook for 3 to 5 minutes undisturbed, then carefully turn. Place a slice of cheese on top of each burger, then cook for a further 5 to 7 minutes until cooked through and firm when pressed.

3 Remove from the heat to rest, then place the bacon on the skillet, cooking until very crisp, along with the onions. Lightly toast the buns, then layer with the burgers, tomatoes, cooked onions and bacon. Serve with mustard and ketchup on the side.

## LOCAL SPECIALITY: THE MANHATTAN

Legend has it that the Manhattan cocktail was invented in the 1860s by a bartender named Black at a bar on Broadway. Traditionalists insist that it should be made with American rye whiskey, but it's frequently made with bourbon or Canadian whiskey.

MAKES ONE SERVING:
1 ¾ fl oz (50ml) American rye whiskey
¾ fl oz (20ml) sweet red vermouth
Dash Angostura bitters
Maraschino cherry to garnish

Stir over ice and strain into a chilled glass. Garnish with the maraschino cherry.

The original New York cheesecake is a rich, creamy baked dessert simply flavored with cream cheese, sour cream and vanilla. No adornment necessary.

# NEW YORK BAKED CHEESECAKE

## Serves 6 – 8

7 oz (200g) graham crackers
   (digestive biscuits), crushed
3 ½ oz (100g) butter
2 ½ oz (70g) superfine (caster)
   sugar
2 tbsp cornstarch (cornflour)
1.2 lb (545g) full fat cream
   cheese
2 eggs
2 ½ fl oz (75ml) sour cream
1 tsp vanilla extract

**1** Grease and line an 8 inch (20cm) springform cake tin and preheat the oven to 350°F (180°C). Make sure that the cream cheese is at room temperature to ensure a smooth finish.

**2** Place the biscuits in a plastic bag and bash with a rolling pin until completely crushed. Melt the butter gently in a saucepan, then mix the two together and press into the base of the tin. Bake the base for 10 minutes, then allow to cool.

**3** Turn the oven up slightly to 400°F (200°C). Mix the sugar and cornstarch together, then using an electric mixer, slowly beat in the cream cheese until smooth. Add the eggs and beat well before adding the sour cream and vanilla extract.

**4** Stand the tin on a couple of sheets of aluminium foil and fold up around the tin, wrapping it so that no water can get in. Spoon the mixture onto the base and smooth the surface. Stand the cheesecake in a baking tray and carefully pour water around it. Bake for 40 to 45 minutes or until golden brown. If the top starts to get too brown, cover loosely with foil. Allow to cool completely before serving.

# CANADA

With its majestic scenery and stunning wildlife, Canada is rich in natural resources. While Canadian cuisine can be viewed as a collage of dishes from other cultures, smoked meat, Pacific salmon and maple syrup are all popular, and French influences in Québec, in particular, have resulted in some exquisite gastronomy.

This indulgent mix of fries, salty cheese curds and gravy is the ultimate French-Canadian comfort food. As it's difficult to track down cheese curds, recreate the dish with a cheese that melts well, like mozzarella or Cheddar.

# POUTINE

## Serves 4

Vegetable oil, for frying
5 large potatoes
2 tbsp butter
2 tbsp all purpose (plain) flour
2 pints (950ml) good quality
   veal or beef stock
8 oz (225g) mozzarella,
   shredded, or Cheddar,
   grated

**1** Peel the potatoes and cut into thick fries. Cover with cold water and allow to soak until needed.

**2** Heat the oil in a deep fat fryer to 375°F (190°C).

**3** Heat the butter in a heavy based frying pan and add the flour. Mix well and allow to cook for a few minutes until pale and bubbling, then gradually whisk in the stock until smooth. Allow to simmer until thick and glossy, whisking frequently.

**4** Drain the fries and pat dry with kitchen paper, then fry in the hot oil until golden and crisp. Drain well, then serve immediately, smothered with the gravy and topped with the shredded cheese.

Originally made with game, this Québecois meat pie is now made with spiced minced pork and beef and traditionally served at Christmas.

# TOURTIÈRE

## Serves 4 – 6

2 tbsp olive oil
1 large onion, finely chopped
1 lb (450g) minced pork
8 oz (225g) minced beef
1 large potato, peeled and
   cut into small dice
½ tsp ground cinnamon
½ tsp ground cloves
Salt and pepper
Nutmeg, grated
6 fl oz (175ml) beef stock

FOR THE PASTRY:

7 oz (200g) cold butter
14 oz (400g) all purpose
   (plain) flour
1 egg + 1 for glazing

**1** Heat the oil in a large, heavy based frying pan and fry the onion for about 10 minutes until soft and lightly golden. Add the pork and beef mince to the pan and combine well, breaking it up and allowing it to brown all over.

**2** Stir in the potato and spices, season well with the salt and pepper and add a generous grating of nutmeg, then pour over the stock. Reduce the heat, cover and simmer for about 30 minutes, stirring occasionally, until most of the liquid is absorbed. Check the seasoning, then allow to cool and refrigerate.

**3** To make the pastry, cut the butter into cubes and place in a bowl with the flour and a pinch of salt. Rub gently with your fingertips until the mixture resembles breadcrumbs. Add the egg and stir gently until the mixture comes together (you may need one or two tablespoons of cold water). Form the dough gently into two balls, wrap and chill for about 20 minutes.

**4** To assemble the pie, first preheat the oven to 375°F (190°C). Roll the pastry out into two discs about ¼ inch (6mm) thick. Use the first circle to line a 9 inch (23cm) pie dish. Add the filling, pressing it down lightly, then cover with the second piece of dough. Wet the edges and crimp all around to seal, then make a small hole at the center of the pie with the tip of a knife.

**5** Whisk the egg, season with salt and pepper and brush generously all over the pie. Bake for an hour until golden brown.

## LOCAL SPECIALITY: TIRE SUR LE NEIGE

Tire sur la neige ('draw on the snow') is an old-fashioned sweet treat in Québec, Canada.

Traditionally, long wooden troughs are filled with snow over which is poured boiled and reduced maple syrup, chilling it to a taffy-like consistency. The taffy is then rolled up on wooden sticks and eaten.

1 quart (32 fl oz) maple syrup
A good amount fresh, clean snow

Bring the maple syrup to a boil in a large saucepan and simmer until it reaches 240°F (116°C) on a candy thermometer. Pour in a thin stream over snow or crushed ice. Let it set for a moment to begin to harden. Roll up on a clean stick.

# THE CARIBBEAN

A colorful blend of turquoise waters,
lush emerald green islands and European
legacies, the islands of the Caribbean are
known for their hot and spicy cuisine.
A fusion of African, Native American,
European, east Indian, Arab and Chinese
influences, Caribbean recipes usually involve
rice, plantains, cilantro, bell peppers,
chickpeas, tomatoes, sweet potatoes and
coconut. But just as every island has its own
distinctive personality, it also has its own
unique recipes.

Part of the amaranth family, callaloo is popular all over the Caribbean.  If you can't find callaloo, substitute spinach or Swiss chard.

# CALLALOO

**Serves 4**

1 lb (450g) fresh Callaloo
2 tbsp vegetable oil
3 garlic cloves, crushed
1 onion, sliced
3 scallions (spring onions),
    chopped
1 sprig of fresh thyme
Salt and black pepper to taste
2 ½ fl oz (75ml) water

**1** Cut any tough stems from the leaves and allow to soak for a few minutes in cold water. Drain, then roughly slice.

**2** Heat the oil in a large saucepan, then add the garlic, onion and scallions. Fry until just beginning to soften, then add the leaves, the sprig of thyme and a generous amount of salt and black pepper. Pour over the water and cover. Cook for about 8 to 10 minutes, stirring occasionally, until the stems are tender. Serve as an accompaniment to jerk chicken.

## LOCAL SPECIALITY: RUM PUNCH

This quintessentially Caribbean cocktail instantly conjures up images of white sand beaches, turquoise sea and that laid-back lifestyle. While many variations of rum punch have evolved over the centuries across the Caribbean, Jamaica is home to the original, with the local people often following the age-old adage 'one of sour, two of sweet, three of strong and four of weak'.

MAKES ONE SERVING:
¾ fl oz (25ml) lime juice
1 ½ fl oz (45ml) sugar cane syrup
2 ¼ fl oz (65ml) dark Jamaican rum
3 fl oz (90ml) water
A sprinkling of freshly grated nutmeg

In a wide glass tumbler, combine all the ingredients over ice cubes and stir well.

To make a larger batch, use the tumbler to measure each ingredient into a jug (one cup of lime juice, two cups of sugar cane syrup, etc).

Jerk cooking probably evolved from a way of smoking and preserving meat used by the Arawak Indians, who settled in Jamaica from South America over 2,500 years ago. Today, Jerk huts selling the spicy, aromatic dish can be found all over the Caribbean.

# JERK CHICKEN

**Serves 4 – 6**

2 scotch bonnet or jalapeño
  chilli peppers, chopped
2 tbsp thyme
1 tbsp ground allspice
4 cloves garlic, chopped
1 tsp fresh ginger, grated
2 tbsp honey
2 tsp salt
2 tsp ground black pepper
1 lime, juiced
1 ½ fl oz (45ml) olive oil
4 chicken breasts, cubed, or 1
  whole chicken, cut into
  pieces

**1** Place all the ingredients apart from the chicken in a blender and process until smooth. Pour the marinade over the chicken and allow to marinate for at least an hour.

**2** Either grill the marinated chicken on a barbecue until cooked through, or bake in the oven at 400°F (200°C) for 25 to 30 minutes, turning half way through the cooking time. Serve immediately with rice 'n' peas.

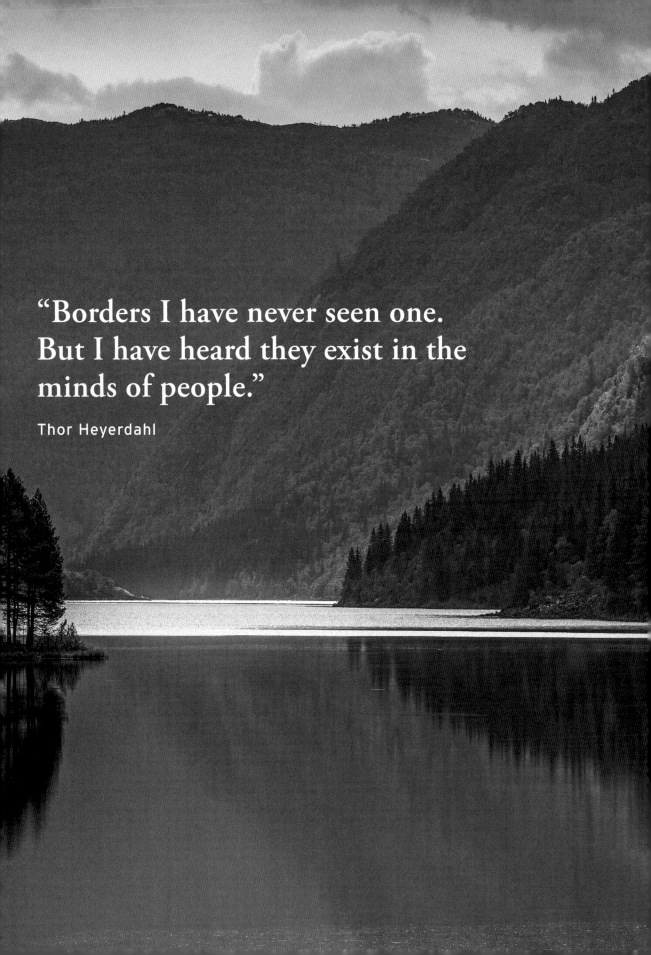

"Borders I have never seen one.
But I have heard they exist in the
minds of people."

Thor Heyerdahl

# COFFEE

Legend has it that coffee was discovered in Ethiopia by a goat herder in the 11th century. He noticed that his goats became energetic and unable to sleep after eating the berries from a certain bush. News of the 'magical' coffee plant soon spread and it wasn't long before Arab traders were bringing the plants home and cultivating them, boiling the beans and drinking the resulting liquid. By the mid-15th century, the Ottoman Turks had brought coffee to Constantinople and before long, Italian traders had introduced it to the West, with the first European coffee houses appearing around 1650.

The ritual of the coffee break is believed to have originated in the late 19th century in Stoughton, Wisconsin in the US, with the wives of Norwegian immigrants taking time away from work to check on their children, and presumably drink coffee. Today, Norway, Finland and the Netherlands are the world's biggest coffee consumers.

Coffee is essentially the national drink in Norway, although Norwegians didn't actually start drinking it until 1694. One theory for its popularity is that it became a substitute for alcohol during Norway's prohibition years between 1916 and 1927. Today, Norway is renowned as a world leader in speciality coffee, and Norwegians enjoy drinking their favorite sort kaffe (black coffee) at cafés and bars as well as at home.

In Sweden, the word *fika* is both a verb and a noun; it's a coffee break, where you sit down to have a cup of coffee and perhaps a sweet roll, and catch up with your friends.

Finnish coffee is the lightest roast in the world, which can be explained by the softness and good quality of Finnish water. And in Finland, the coffee break is compulsory.

Denmark's café culture is hugely popular and intrinsically linked to the concept of *hygge*, a sense of wellbeing, cosiness and spending time with loved ones. A visit to a coffee shop is a chance to escape the cold and stay for a while, rather than just a quick caffeine hit.

Green coffee was being imported and roasted in Iceland by the mid-18th century and was originally served on high days and holidays. By the end of the 19th century, coffee was truly part of everyday life, with a huge amount being consumed by the small island.

In 17th century England, coffee began to be imported by the East India Company and coffee houses sprang up, becoming dens of subversive religious and political talk – so much so that Charles II attempted to ban them.

Italians usually drink coffee standing up (sitting down costs more money), never order a cappuccino after 11am and like to keep their coffee orders simple.

Similarly, in Portugal, there's a coffee shop on every corner and espresso or bica is hugely popular, especially served with *pastéis de nata*, the popular local pastry. The most popular way to drink coffee in Spain, especially in the morning, is *café con leche* – half coffee and half milk.

Coffee is seen as an art form in Austria and coffee houses in its capital Vienna are elegant gathering places. Similarly in Switzerland, *milchkafi* (milky coffee) and cake in one of the historic coffee houses is a weekend institution.

Considered a drink only for nobility in 17th century Germany, today *kaffee und kuchen*, or coffee and cake, is a popular Sunday afternoon ritual, which shows the importance of the beverage to Germans.

In Eastern Europe, the first cafés began to appear in places like Warsaw, Poland, in the mid-17th century. Having fallen out of favor during the communist era, the café culture is now once again popular. The Czech Republic celebrates its coffee with an annual Coffee Festival.

Turkey's unique method of brewing its coffee produces a delicious aroma and is actually the basis for most of the coffee drunk in Arab countries today.

Although Greece has also embraced contemporary coffee culture, traditional Greek coffee, *ellinikós kafés* – a slightly lighter version of Turkish coffee, is still found everywhere.

In Asia, although you'll find coffee growing all over Burma (Myanmar), you're unlikely to find anything other than instant coffee and are much more likely to be served fresh green tea in restaurants, or black tea in tea houses. In Cambodia, though, new coffee shops and cafés are springing up all over the more modern cities like Phnom Penh.

While China is mostly associated with the production of tea, there's also a growing industry of coffee production. The younger generation are embracing coffee consumption, and hundreds of Starbucks are springing up in major cities. China certainly has some catching up to do, however, with the national average being just four cups per person per year.

Vietnam's French heritage means that coffee is incredibly popular in cities such as Ho Chi Minh and Hanoi, although the classic Vietnamese coffee known as *ca phe sua da*, made with sweetened condensed milk and ice, can take some getting used to.

In the USA, free refills of coffee come as standard, but despite the fact that Starbucks was founded in Seattle, and the US is the largest market for coffee, Americans don't consume as much coffee as one might imagine, instead preferring to go for quality over quantity.

Canadians, too, love their coffee, with 14 billion cups consumed in Canada every year, and new independent coffee shops and small batch roasters appearing all the time.

The fertile islands of the Caribbean means that coffee beans grown near Jamaica's majestic Blue Mountains are widely regarded as some of the best in the world.

Puerto Rico, the Dominican Republic and Haiti, are currently experiencing a resurgence in the coffee trade after the devastating earthquake of 2010, and all produce excellent coffee. Good news for a world that now consumes over 2.25 billion cups of coffee every day.

COFFEE
191

# WINE

'Wine can of their wits the wise beguile, make the sage frolic, and the serious smile' according to Homer's *Odyssey*.

History is full of mentions of civilizations like the Egyptians and the Phoenicians making a wine-like substance from fermenting grapes. Around 1200BC, when the Phoenicians started to trade across the Mediterranean to the Middle East, Greece and Italy, they brought their wine with them. As the Greeks began to colonize more land, so they planted their grape vines and perfected their craft. By the time the Romans conquered the Greeks, they'd adopted wine into their culture; as the Roman Empire adopted the Catholic Church, so the knowledge of wine grew and spread across Europe, reaching the New World with the Conquistadors by the 15th century. The rest, as they say, is history, but travelers and adventurers continued to bring and plant vines, and a global industry was created. In fact, the only continent that doesn't now grow grapes is Antarctica.

France produces a huge range of different wines due to its wide range of climates. From the cool, northerly Champagne region producing delicious, dry bubbles, to the continental climate of Burgundy (now merged with its eastern neighbor, Franche-Comté); the fresh Atlantic coastline of Bordeaux, down to the dry southeastern Rhône-Alpes, and the Mediterranean heat of Provence and the Languedoc (now joined by Midi-Pyrénées) producing delicious Provencal rosés, the French will continue to be the world's largest wine producer.

Dating back to ancient Roman times and mostly situated in the Rhine regions, vineyards in Germany produce high quality wines, mainly the aromatic white Reisling.

In Italy, where '*il vino fa buon sangue*', which literally means 'good wine makes good blood', the ancient vineyards are home to over 2,000 grape varieties. Each region has its own very distinct style of wine; elegant Brunello and Chianti from Tuscany, Piedmont's 'King of Wines', Barolo, and the vastly popular Prosecco from Veneto.

From being more well known for its fortified wines: Port and Madeira, and the fresh, green Vinho Verde of the cool northwest, the terraced vineyards of the Douro valley in Portugal have come to the fore with their incredible rich, ripe reds.

As varied as the landscape and climate, Spain produces a huge diversity of wines: from Tempranillo, famous for producing the deep, ruby Rioja to citrussy, white Albariño.

As one of the oldest wine producing countries in the world, Greece's wine industry has stayed surprisingly small, although Greek wines are slowly beginning to gain popularity. The minerally whites produced in tiny Santorini are particularly worth seeking out.

Although evidence suggests that vineyards were planted in China thousands of years ago, it's really only been within living memory that drinking wine has gained any popularity in Asia. A couple of Chinese Cabernet Sauvignons and some great quality dessert wines have started to emerge. Not to be left out, Cambodia has started to produce Khmer red wine.

Vines were introduced to Mexico and Brazil back in the 15th century by the conquistadors and soon spread across South America. Spanish missionaries traveled south, establishing Chile's first winery in Mendoza in the mid-16th century, and north, bringing grapes from Mexico to the USA. California still produces five times more wine than the total of the other most popular regions: New York, Oregon and Washington. Sonoma and Napa's lush, fruit-forward Cabernet Sauvignon continue to have worldwide appeal.

And in the future? As well as sipping reds from China and whites from the Czech Republic, we'll be drinking fabulous wines from Michigan and Texas and delicate fizz from Franciacorta in Italy. We probably shouldn't hold our breath for that Chardonnay from Antarctica.

# BEER

In Belgium, beer was originally brewed in abbeys, where the craft was developed. Heavy taxes on French wines traditionally created a demand for Belgian beer. Although 60 percent is now exported, cafés all across Belgium serve a wide selection of beers, from the darkest of ales to the pale, cloudy and scented witbier.

France also produces a number of excellent beers: a small amount in Brittany, but mostly in the Alsace-Lorraine region, and with its cultural ties to Belgium, the Nord-Pas-de-Calais region, traditionally producing golden, malty Bière de Garde.

Germany's beer production is legendary, with over 5,000 different beers currently in production and beer consumption per head only trumped by the Czechs.

Austria is a huge consumer of beer and the Upper Austrian region of Mühlviertel, north of the Danube, is home to a wealth of breweries all producing fine Austrian beers.

Not typically known for its wine production, hardier vine varieties are starting to experience some success in Scandinavia. Beer, on the other hand, has been brewed in Norway since the Vikings were creating ale back in the 12th century, and Norwegian craft beer is gaining serious notoriety. In Denmark, giants Carlsberg dominate the market, but microbreweries are emerging in Denmark and Sweden too.

And although the eastern region of Moravia is having increasing success with wine production, the Czech Republic is the world's biggest consumers of beer. From the creation of the first pilsners to today's culture of beer spas and even beer hotels, beer is a huge part of Czech culture. There are breweries dotted all across the country, and across neighboring Slovakia, from huge household names to tiny microbreweries, brewing much more than just the typical pale lagers the Czechs are famed for.

# DIGESTIFS

## ARMAGNAC

The oldest brandy distilled in France, Armagnac takes its name from the region in Gascony where it has made since the 14th century. Unlike Cognac, which is distilled twice, Armagnac is distilled only once. Traditionally served after dinner, Armagnac can be paired with a variety of desserts. Torshavn, the piano lounge on board Viking Cruises ocean ships, offers the broadest collection of fine vintage Armagnacs at sea.

## SAUTERNES

Sauternes is a French sweet wine made from grapes that have been affected by a fungus called *botrytis cinerea*, also known as noble rot. This causes the grapes to become partially raisined, resulting in distinct and concentrated flavors. Due to its climate, Sauternes is one of the few wine regions where noble rot is a frequent occurrence. The wines are typically served chilled at 52°F (11°C) with older wines served a few degrees warmer.

## LIMONCELLO

Best enjoyed while dining al fresco on a warm summer's evening, limoncello is a refreshing Italian lemon liqueur traditionally served ice-cold in small, chilled glasses.

7 large lemons
1 liter (1.1 litre) high proof neutral alcohol
1 liter (1.1 litre) water
1.5 lb (700g) sugar

1 Using a vegetable peeler, remove the zest from the lemons. Place the zest in a large jar and pour in the alcohol. Allow to infuse at room temperature for at least 48 hours.

2 After the infusion period, strain the contents of the jar through muslin, catching the yellow liquid in a bowl. Next, boil the water and add the sugar, stirring until dissolved, and allow to cool. Strain the syrup through muslin like before. Combine the yellow liquid with the syrup, stir well, pour into clean bottles and chill in the freezer before serving.

"The first condition of understanding
a foreign country is to smell it."

Rudyard Kipling

# INDEX

"So throw off the bowlines. Sail away from the safe harbor. Catch the trade winds in your sails. Explore. Dream. Discover."

Mark Twain

**First published in Germany in 2016 by Viking Cruises**

**Copyright © Viking Cruises 2016**

ISBN 978-1-909968-15-8

Book design by The Chelsea Magazine Company Limited

Photography: James Murphy, Alistair Miller.
Additional images: AWL Images, Corbis Images,
Getty Images, iStock.

Recipe testing: Rebecca Wiggins

Printed and bound in Germany by Mohn Media

**Viking Cruises**
83 Wimbledon Park Side
London SW19 5LP

**www.vikingcruises.co.uk**